P9-DEP-895

Lift Every Voice

Dr. Walter Turnbull,

FOUNDER AND DIRECTOR OF THE BOYS CHOIR OF HARLEM

with Howard Manly

HYPERION

New York

Lift Every Voice

EXPECTING
THE MOST
AND
GETTING
THE BEST
FROM ALL
OF GOD'S
CHILDREN

"The Sundays of Satin-Legs Smith" on pages 107–108 Copyright © Gwendolyn Brooks, reprinted from *Blacks*, published by David Company, 1987.

Copyright © 1995, Dr. Walter Turnbull

All rights reserved. No part of this book may be used or reproduced in any manner whatsoever without the written permission of the Publisher. Printed in the United States of America. For information address: Hyperion, 114 Fifth Avenue, New York, New York 10011.

Library of Congress Cataloging-In-Publication Data

Turnbull, Walter J.
    Lift every voice : expecting the most and getting the best from all of God's children / by Walter Turnbull, with Howard Manly.
        p. cm.
    ISBN 0-7868-6164-9
    1. Turnbull, Walter J.   2. Afro-American choral conductors—Biography.   3. Boys Choir of Harlem.   4. Self-esteem in children.
5. Child development.   I. Manly, Howard, 1957–   II. Title.
ML422.T87A3 1995
782.7'09747'1—dc20   95-36920
                                                       CIP
                                                       MN

Designed by Claudyne Bianco

FIRST EDITION

10 9 8 7 6 5 4 3 2 1

To Steven Sims and Horace Turnbull:
Their unshakable support nourished
my soul and kept joy in the Boys Choir
of Harlem.

Acknowledgments

FIRST AND FOREMOST, I thank God for giving me the "Gift of Song." To Martha Patterson and the Boys Choir of Harlem staff, especially my right-hand man, Frank Jones, Jr., for their continued support. To Yolanda Toby for being a true friend. To those who have encouraged me personally: Joanie and Nick Danielides, McCall Credle, and Betsy Levin. To members of the Marketing Committee, which the late Barry Rosenthall established: Gail Hamilton, Bill Preston, and Rick Levin. To those board members whose faith in my work was unshakable. To the Boys Choir of Harlem parents, whose prayers have sustained me over the years. To the Tougaloo College family and especially Mr. Clarence Hunter at the Zenobia Coleman Library, Mr. Larry Robinson, Dr. Ben Bailey, the Honorable Constance Slaughter, and my classmates, Dr. Dora Wilson and Mr. Robert Honeysucker. To all of the New Yorkers who rallied to my aid after a fire in my apartment destroyed all of my material things. To my aunt Florida Jackson, my uncle James Turnbull, and cousin Dr. Matthew Page for coming through in the clutch.

A special thanks to John Taylor Williams and Lane Zachary of the Palmer and Dodge Literary Agency; and to Pat Mulcahy, whose gentle nudges and delicate editing qualifies her for sainthood. And finally to Howard Manly, his parents, Theresa and Howard Manly, and his colleagues Rick Hyde, Eric Grant, Ellen Clegg, Mike Barnicle, Stan Grossfeld, Greg Moore, Stacey Kabat, Michele McPhee, Robert Vickerman, Charles M. Sennott, Rose DeVine, Miles Shapiro, Barbara Heffernan, and Tammy Manly. His wife, Sharon, and their three children Rachel, Chandler, and Wren, gave him the love to persevere throughout the project, and for that I am in their debt. And of course, Wil Haygood, who inspired, and Gloria and Carl Chandler, who baby-sat while Howard claimed he was writing a book.

Prologue

I HAVE LISTENED to voices in Harlem for the last twenty-six years, and though many are among the sweetest in the world, the stories behind the talent are often quite painful and remarkable. When I started the Boys Choir of Harlem twenty-six years ago, I did not set out to establish an internationally known performance group. I simply wanted to share the joy of music with African-American children. It has the kind of power to lift people above any particular circumstance and inspire the heart. Music is very magical, able to transform children with no more than lint in their pockets and honey in their throats into grand performers on the world stage. Perfection in music demands discipline and instills self-confidence, two virtues easily transferred beyond the arts to everyday life. I am fifty-one years old now, and that is what I know. Music took me from the Mississippi cotton fields to prestigious performance centers all over the world. My childhood may have been different from the one children experience nowadays in New

York City. But we share poverty and a sense of hope and a desire for better things to come. I still have faith that music has lost none of its ability to transform.

Yuseff Washington provides a little evidence. I did not know anything about him when we first met at P.S. 11. He was one of about two hundred elementary school children auditioning one morning in 1986 to become members of the Boys Choir of Harlem. I had about three hours to listen and make a decision on whether a child had the right kind of voice. The tryout was basic: students were asked to sing anything that came to their minds. Some sang Christmas carols. Others sang songs by Stevie Wonder. I then played a scale on the piano and asked them to repeat what they heard. Yuseff had a quite lovely voice and a good ear. Based on those talents, I invited him to join the boys choir as a student. We talked with his grandmother, his legal guardian at the time, and his story began to unfold.

From all appearances, Yuseff Washington was an outgoing, smart child but, through no fault of his own, he was the product of a broken home, struggling on the fringes of American society. He is seventeen years old now and has blocked out the behavior of the adults in his life, preferring instead to view them through the prism of survival: they simply did what they had to do. The imperfections began with his father. Yuseff still does not know his real name: "It's J.L. or something like that," he says. Either way, Yuseff has never met him, and the likelihood of such a meeting is long gone. His father died several years ago. "I remember seeing pictures of him," Yuseff says. "I really couldn't make them out because he had a thick beard. But everybody says I look just like him. People who knew him will stop me in the street and say, 'You J.L.'s boy.' " One of his mother's friends told Yuseff that his father had died from cancer.

That friend did not know where "J.L. or something" was buried and, to this day, neither does Yuseff.

Yuseff grew up in Harlem, fatherless, and for the most part, motherless. It never really bothered him—he never knew anything different. His mother raised him as best she could until her use of crack squeezed her maternal instincts from her soul. She had no problem waking up her child in the middle of the night to walk to the corner grocery store. When the urge hit her, she squatted between two parked cars or in darkened alleys and told Yuseff to warn her of passersby. On the rare ocassions that she stayed at home, she locked herself in the bathroom for as many as six hours, most of the time passed out, leaving Yuseff and his younger brother virtually alone. For a while, when Yuseff was about seven years old, an older brother and sister lived in the tiny apartment on 115th Street and Seventh Avenue and could provide the basics. That meant as long as the youngsters were alive in the morning, everything was all right. The older siblings had their own hankering for the streets, and little things just got by them. Like the time Yuseff saw a piece of cheese lying on the floor near the corner of his living room. Unfortunately, the cheese sat on a rattrap, and when Yuseff grabbed the cheese, his fingers triggered the metal snap. The pain lasted seemingly for hours; the mark on his pinky finger is permanent.

By the middle of Yuseff's third-grade year, he had missed fifty-five days of classes. Yuseff was eight years old then and had become his four-year-old brother's de facto guardian. They sat around the apartment, all day and all night, watching television and listening to music. Yuseff could cook a little, but for the most part, food was an issue. Both of them felt perfectly comfortable knocking on neighbors' doors around dinnertime when they were hungry. As far as they knew, that was what all children did. Sometimes, the neighbors were nice and invited them in to sit down at their table; other times the children would beg until the neighbors at least gave them a sandwich or a few cookies. The number of absences gave school administrators a red flag. They told the city Bureau of Child Services, which immediately dispatched several of their social workers to Yuseff's apartment. For the next several days, Yuseff, his older sister, and younger brother lived in shelters until the city agency could find a foster home. Yuseff stayed with a family in Queens for a while. Yuseff's grandmother gained custody of the three children in time for Yuseff's fourth-grade year.

The majority of the children that attend the Boys Choir have stories simliar to Yuseff's. More than 75 percent of our children come from single-parent households headed by females. Once they are accepted into our school, we in effect help raise the child and provide male role models. We accepted Yuseff, knowing full well that he was still developing as an individual. He has been with us ever since. He still has some of the ugliness left over from his upbringing. Instead of simply asking for what he wants, he has a habit of trying to manipulate people. He lives on the surface and sees himself as very transient. But our focus here is on forgiveness. We work on the premise that people are good, and given the right set of circumstances, they will choose to be and do good. The relationship between the adults and the children is one of kinship. The bond here is unlike the one established at most other schools, where a form of indebtedness exists: the teacher gives the student something, and the student gives the teacher something back in return. If the child does something wrong, he is punished and, in many cases, left behind.

The currency here is a sense of security. We do not abandon children just because they have low grades or are not selected to perform on tour. We believe in them, and our attitude causes the children to believe in us and what we are trying to accomplish. For Yuseff, the Boys Choir of Harlem represents the first real sense of stability that he has ever had. We are the one constant in his life. He knows that we care about him, regardless of the manner of his upbringing. We cannot help every child, but the ones that we do—and there have been thousands—leave here with a sense that they are part of something larger than themselves. At first, it's the Boys Choir of Harlem, and later, American society.

In his seminal volume *On the Teaching of Children*, the great Greek educator Plutarch wrote, "The very spring and root of honesty and virtue lie in a good education." Those words have lost none of their applicability nearly two thousand years later. What has changed, though maybe not nearly as much as we might imagine, is the challenge of instilling those important qualities—honesty, virtue, hope, courage, and integrity—in today's youth. Especially African-American youth, who have been failed over and over again, sometimes by our educational system, sometimes by the media, sometimes, as in Yuseff's case, by their own parents, and sometimes, sadly, by themselves. Talk with any teacher, white or black, any principal or school administrator, and you will hear the same complaints: too few teachers for too many kids; too few after-school programs to provide alternatives to the lure of of the streets; the numbing influence of television and video games; too many teachers too willing to give up on their students and too many students too willing to give up on themselves. It does not have to be this way.

The idea of having a boys choir is nothing new. It is a form of ministry almost a millennium old. In Europe, after Rome fell and the light went out on learning and the arts for hundreds of years, the Church was the guardian of all that remained of Greaco-Roman society. In most places, monks and priests were the only people who could read and write. The church was more than the center of spiritual life; it was the center of all life. All duchies had a chapel of men and boys. Music existed mostly to give greater glory to God, and one of the highest forms of art was the pure, ethereal sound of the boys' voices. The brightest and most talented boys were chosen, given an education, lodged, and fed under the auspices of the church. It was an honor to be chosen for the chapel boys choir. As time passed, the relationship of the Church to the arts changed, but the status of the choir never did. Our other inspiration is the African-American church. It has been a great source of power in the black community, beginning with the secret worshiping that slaves practiced in the hush of night, through the Civil Rights movement, when black preachers used the pulpit to galvanize a nation. The songs of freedom and joy, of pain and suffering, reflect the black experience.

My childhood was not easy—but the children growing up in Harlem today have such a seemingly more difficult way to go. I have tried to figure out the differences. My times had been hard, and there was prejudice aplenty growing up in Greenville, Mississippi, in the forties and fifties—before the Civil Rights movement. But I always had something: hope, faith, a sense of self-worth, and love. I had the usual household chores, but I also had music. Talent coupled with a desire to be the best prevented me from succumbing to peer pressure and hanging out in the streets. I was too busy polishing what I considered a God-given gift. I wanted to be somebody. Whenever I performed, in church or onstage, people reacted and encouraged me to persevere. I worked hard. My efforts made me feel good and gave me the courage to try new things. In both high school and college, I was a student leader, elected president of the student governments, glee clubs, and choirs. I learned to establish goals, work hard, and achieve my goals. That drive enabled me to graduate from college and later receive a master's degree and a doctorate, both from the Manhattan School of Music.

But fires of the heart are not lit in one day. I started with two friends of mine, Marcus and Lonieta Thompson, by going to my elders at the Ephesus Church of Central Harlem and asking for their permission to start a boys choir at the church. They approved the idea and we held auditions and picked twenty boys. We began in the basement of the church. Never in my wildest imagination would I dream that twenty years later, the choir would have its own school—the Boys Choir of Harlem Academy—to serve boys and girls ages four to eighteen and grades four through twelve. I didn't know that our school would grow, providing 450 young men and women the finest elementary, junior high, and high school education that we can offer. We were called the Ephesus Boys Choir of Central Harlem then, and I certainly did not know that we would become a truly American cultural institution.

We have performed at some of the country's most auspicious occasions: the rededication of the Statue of Liberty, Nelson Mandela's arrival in the United States after he obtained his freedom from his long imprisonment in South Africa, and the five hundredth anniversary of Columbus's arrival in America. We have performed for presidents at the White House, had our own show on Broadway, and graced the stages of some of the world's finest performing venues and historic churchs—from Radio City Music Hall, Carnegie Hall, and the Apollo Theatre in New York to the Budokan in Tokyo, St. Paul's Cathedral in London, and Notre Dame in Paris. Our voices have been heard on movie soundtracks such as *Glory*, *Malcolm X*, and *Jungle Fever*. Our media coverage has been exceptional, especially considering the preponderance of newspaper and television accounts of the exploits of drug dealers and misogynist rappers. We have been the subject of thousands of stories showing the other side of the African-American community, the one where young brothers and sisters are in fact working hard and trying to do the right thing.

Hard work is the key to success at the Boys Choir of Harlem. As choir members quickly discover, I will not tolerate putting one member's needs above the good of the group. Bad behavior will simply not be accepted, nor will selfishness. Furthermore, a student must earn the right to be a member of the choir. There are about two hundred young men who constitute our Concert Choir; of these, thirty-five or forty are chosen to be a part of the Performing Choir, the group that is on television and stage. A great voice and good looks are not enough. Superior academic performance, an excellent attendance record, and commitment to constant improvement are all equally important criteria. Unlike in too many of our nation's sports programs, winning isn't everything. There is no good reason to give the spotlight to a student, no matter how great his natural abilities, who is unwilling to better himself in every way.

Parental involvement is the other key to success. You hardly need to have studied Freud or read Shakespeare or Aeschylus to know that deep down every child wishes to have his or her parents' approval. In today's world, not every child has a functioning biological parent. Some have legal guardians, which might be a grandmother or an uncle or a foster parent. In some cases, I have become a father of sorts to many of the children. Despite their protestations to the contrary, I find that most children wish that their parents—or surrogate parents—would pay more attention to their lives and their behavior, even if that means setting rules or enforcing discipline. Children want to please those they respect. Unlike perfunctory parent-teacher conferences or calling Mom to the principal's office to discuss bad behavior, the choir provides an atmosphere for parents and students to come together. We encourage parents to get involved in many ways, more than simply coming to performances or rehearsals. The academy has a counseling unit for students and families, a service that many take advantage of. Moreover, if we see the need for parental involvement, we ask. As we tell our students, you can't just wait for things to happen; you have to make things happen. If we need to pick up the telephone once, twice, or even three times to get a parent over to the school, we call.

The results speak for themselves. I could not be prouder of the many boys who have graduated from the choir and gone on to productive, successful lives in any number of fields: business, education, law, medicine, religion, and, yes, even music. I am also proud of the fact that 98 percent of the choir's alumni have gone on to college. That is a remarkable achievement for any high school, public or private, and especially considering that in 1993, only 34 percent of black students went on to college, and even sadder, that 30 percent of black students drop out of high school altogether. What we have accomplished is extraordinary.

Lift
Every
Voice

Mississippi Roots

I **WAS BORN** in Greenville, Mississippi, but my story begins deeper in the Delta, about fifteen miles away, in a little town named Longswitch. It's not really a town now, just a name left over from the point on the map where the Illinois Central trains, connecting New Orleans to Chicago, switched tracks. If you take the highway north from Greenville, past the rolling fields and the old cotton gin near Dunleith Road, you will come to a small bridge that crosses a dirty brown-colored stream. Make a left onto the one-lane road, cross the railroad tracks, and round the gentle curve. The four weathered houses, their wood panels missing chunks of white paint, are the last buildings remaining from the days when scores of colored laborers and share-croppers lived on the fringes of the plantations—and, for that matter, the fringes of America.

The meager building that served as the Cato Baptist Church is gone, as is the once busy general store. Most days the only sounds that break the sleepy quiet are the ones coming from crickets, a few dogs, and a herd of cattle up the road a bit. A strong wind across these seemingly endless flat fields, dotted with only a few pine trees separating one plantation from another, disrupts the quiet like a siren in the night. In these fields lie buried my maternal grandparents. They rest in a family-owned plot of land where there are no markers or headstones, no epitaphs or flowers. They are simply covered by the same rich Delta soil that they worked until they died.

Like that of most blacks, our family history can be traced back two or three generations to slavery. Go back any further and our roots vanish into the Atlantic Ocean. The damnable business of selling human flesh destroyed our footprints, leaving behind only finely scripted bills of sale, filed away in dusty journals kept in southern courthouses. Slave traders and plantation owners reduced our culture and souls to statistics: height, weight, and sex. Nothing was written down for us, just passed along in stories told around the wood-burning stove, and when that storyteller died, so, too, did the details.

My family history can only be stitched together like some sort of patchwork quilt of memories—a story here, a date there. My father's sister and two brothers remember a few things. My cousin, Dr. Matthew Page, remembers more. Though the details are fuzzy, one thing is indisputable: from the very beginning, we were at the bottom. What little education we received was earned either at the handle of a hoe or at the end of a whip. The two constants were hard work and an unwavering belief that, somehow, the Lord would deliver us from the strange form of democracy practiced along the Delta. We had faith in a life that we could not see.

It is hard for me to imagine my ancestors' journey from

Africa to America. The men were shackled two by two, the right wrist and ankle of one chained to the left wrist and ankle of another. They slept in the hold without covering on bare wooden floors in spaces no bigger than tailor-made coffins. In a stormy passage, the skin over their elbows might be worn away to the bone. The crew allowed the women to roam freely throughout the ship. They were fair game. By the end of the Middle Passage, more often than not, the living were chained to the dead. Not too long ago, I visited the slave castles in Ghana, the buildings where slavers herded their human cattle and shipped them through what the Africans called "the Door of No Return." More than four hundred years later, I could still smell the stench in the dungeons. Seeing those castles had a profound effect on me, and when I teach children about man's inhumanity to man and the importance of having common decency for one another, I think of the chains rustling along the dungeon floors. I often tell students that their problems pale in comparison: the remains of at least eleven million of their ancestors lie on the bottom of the Atlantic Ocean.

My paternal great-grandfather, Woodley Turnbull, was a slave. It is not clear whether he was born en route or on American soil, but he died in 1929 and lived to be 106 or 107 years old. No one really knows for sure how old he was because there was no birth certificate, just speculation based on geography and the names of white men. Either way, his dark brown skin and sinewy arms and legs determined that he was a commodity, something to be bought and sold on the open market. If he couldn't read the section of the U.S. Constitution spelling out that he was only worth three fifths of a human being, then his master constantly reminded him.

3

My father's brother, James, lived with Woodley Turnbull in Detroit, shortly before he died. Great-grandpa Woodley was old and fragile, and Uncle James was a little boy then. The conversations between the two were brief: Uncle James not knowing what to ask, and Pa Woodley wanting to spare a young mind the details of his life, filled with "do this and do that." "Sometimes he would get a licking if he didn't move fast enough," Uncle James recalled his grandfather telling him. "Other times he got a licking just 'cuz."

Woodley Turnbull was somewhat fortunate—he had "a good master." The white Turnbulls were very wealthy and close to the English crown. They had petitioned the queen for land in the colonies before the American Revolution and had plantations in Virginia, the Carolinas, and in the Caribbean. Most of the Turnbulls were among the professional class as well—doctors and lawyers—and were considered to be combination planters. They traded their crops and properties among themselves, and for the most part, if they sold a slave, they tried to keep his family intact. That practice has had a lasting effect and can be seen in the similar facial and physical features of Turnbulls spread throughout America and the Caribbean. For instance, Dr. Charles Turnbull, the former minister of education in the Virgin Islands, could be my uncle. Another Turnbull, who now plays professional football for the New Orleans Saints, also shows a strong resemblance, but we have not established any blood kinship yet. Regardless of the white Turnbulls' peculiar notion of family, they remained businessmen. They chased dollars, not members of my family taken from the Ibo and Yoruba tribes.

That chase led to the Delta. The Turnbulls, like many other cotton planters, had exhausted their farms along the east coast. Some went to Texas and Louisiana. Others became so frantic for new land that they were ready to risk the hardship and fevers of the swamplands along the Mississippi River. Those fertile lands, straddling the Arkansas and Mississippi borders, were brimming with forests of oak and beech, hickory and maple, walnut and cypress, and alive with bear and deer, possum and squirrel. Doves and quail flew everywhere. The land that would eventually become Washington County was the most fertile in the region. But it was largely impenetrable: the forests were too thick, the diseases too rampant, the floods too frequent. Black panthers roamed freely on land, poisonous snakes flourished along the rivers and creeks. Not even the Choctaw or Chickasaw Indians settled in the area. They used it only for an occasional hunting party or as ceremonial burial grounds. One planter visited the area and urged his colleagues not to move there. He thought the slaves would surely die off in a few years from fever and overwork.

River pirates were the first white settlers. As historian Bern Keating tells the story, they lurked on islands and preyed on flatboats carrying produce from northern farms to market in New Orleans. Law-abiding Christians finally chased them out and pleaded with the federal government to work out an agreement with the Choctaws. The Treaty of Doak's Stand, signed in 1820, put the federal stamp on the inevitable westward rush from the Atlantic seaboard. It's unclear who was the first to settle in Washington County, but by 1827, Frederick Turnbull was one of the 170 names that appeared on the tax rolls for property owners. Forty-one of them owned between one to thirty-six slaves. The tax assessor's list also shows one "Free Man of Color." My great-grandfather, his real name lost somewhere between the slave auction in South Carolina and the Mississippi River, was not that man and, more than likely, accepted his hand-me-down name with the same enthusiasm as he did his station in life.

Clearing the forests and taming the Mississippi River required enormous labor and fortitude. Though the region was only for the rich planters, few lived in their usual style of verandas and columns. They usually came into the jungle with a gang of slaves, cleared a homesite, and built a log cabin. If the site was near the banks of the Mississippi River, they came to the banks by steamboat. If it was inland, they poled their way up the bayous by raft. Most families lived in log cabins with dirt floors. They suffered from hordes of mosquitoes bred in the swamps, and they shivered and ached all summer with the same malaria that attacked the poorest slaves. One writer at the time observed that the slaves in the Delta died in a few years, but the rich soil made enough money to replace them twice over. By 1829, Washington County contained 792 whites, 1,184 slaves, and one "Free Man of Color." The county included a little hamlet called Greenville, named after Revolutionary War hero Nathanael Greene, a close friend of George Washington. Inventories of estates in county court records show that the most valuable properties were young strong male slaves. They averaged $500 in value. One little slave boy was valued at only $3.50. That was probably Woodley Turnbull. He would have been about six or seven then, uneducated, and barely able to speak the language.

Landowners were making progress, though. Within two years, 324 acres had been cleared and were on the tax rolls. The white population dropped during those years, from 223 to 202, and the number of slaves had tripled to 3,196. Within four years, the landowners had lost the nerve of the pioneers and chose to run their plantations from afar, leaving overseers in charge. By 1846, the county's white population had fallen about 20 percent from the 1830 count, but there were five times as many slaves, a trend that continued until the Civil War and caused many troubled nights among the rich and powerful. Though they owned most of the weapons, slave owners still had fresh memories of Denmark Vesey's uprising in 1822 in South Carolina, or Nat Turner's rebellion in Virginia in 1831 with its body count of seventy whites.

I'm not sure where my great-grandfather stood on slave rebellions. He was deeply religious and would later tell my uncle that his fate during slavery was in the hands of the Lord. Freedom must have been as remote a prayer as his native homeland in Africa. The cluster of slave cabins surrounded the fringes of the plantation, where masters and overseers could watch every movement. At night, overseers and bounty hunters, armed with guns, whips, dogs, and the power of the state, patrolled the community for slaves crazy enough to even whisper the word "freedom." One law read:

Patrol has the authority to arrest all slaves going at large and away from owner's property without written permission of owner (or his agent) after 9 P.M. Punishment authorized for runaway slaves 39 lashes or confinement in jail. Patrol authorized to enter after 9 P.M. the premises of Negro quarters of any person in the district to locate runaways, but only in a peaceable, orderly and quiet manner. When a slave represents himself to have been sent for a physician or for medicine, the patrol is to accompany him on the errand and to establish the truth or falsehood of the Negro's statement. In case of falsehood he was to be whipped as a runaway.

There was no option but to believe in something other than man, and God, not the North Star leading up North or to Canada, was the brightest star my great-grandfather could see.

Plantation owners had by the 1840s allowed slaves to have their own churches. Many slaves, who had tried to learn the words and hymns of their owners, were now able to worship as they saw fit. Still, they had to hide their African language and culture. Freedom, at least in terms of the law, would come after the Civil War. The Washington County delegation to the Mississippi Convention in 1861 voted against secession, but once overruled by other state delegations, the members threw the state into the war with the fervor of any other fire breathers from the Deep South. Ann Finlay lived in Greenville, and one of her letters describing life during that time was recounted in Bern Keating's *History of Washington County, Mississippi*: "Mississippi seceded; drums began to beat, men and boys to drill, and orators to pour out all their eloquence for the new cause. Men were putting their affairs in shape to go to the front, businesses were almost forgotten, every nerve was strained to the utmost." When Union soldiers made their way to Greenville, the locals put up little resistance before seeing their hamlet burned to the ground.

The national confusion over the institution of slavery spilled over into the slave community. On the eve of the Civil War, a census showed 1,212 whites and 14,467 slaves in Washington County. Some slaves joined the Union Army, others joined the Confederate Army. And still others, like Woodley, simply struck out on their own, running away from their plantations and floating up the Mississippi River. He eventually settled in a small Mississippi town named Bourbon. He carried his Bible and his farming skills, and somehow managed to eke out a living. No matter the suffering, he believed, life on earth was only a tick on God's clock; heaven was an eternity. The Lord was never far away, Woodley told my Uncle James, and he often went to the banks of the Mississippi and read, as best he could, his favorite biblical verse:

> By the waters of Babylon, there we sat down, yea, we wept when we remembered Zion. We hanged our harps upon the willows in the midst thereof. For there they that carried us away captive required of us a song. And they that wasted of us required us mirth, saying, "Sing us one of the songs of Zion." How shall we sing the Lord's song in a strange land.

Woodley sat on the bottom rail of society, and from his vantage point, America was indeed a stranger place after the Civil War and the Emancipation Proclamation. He was a slave one minute, free the next, but in the eyes of most white southerners, still less than a man. His dark skin was a badge of servitude, a guarantee that he had no rights—at least none that the white man was bound to respect. "Ours is and ever shall be a government for white men," Governor Benjamin Humphreys promised Mississippi in his 1865 inaugural address. The onerous Black Codes, passed by the state legislature, were the result. If the Thirteenth Amendment abolished slavery, the codes all but replaced it.

Woodley's response was silence. He may have lost his culture but he surely had not lost his mind. Speaking against the codes was a crime, as was carrying a gun or a knife for a black man. Insulting a white man or preaching without a license was punishable by thirty days in jail and a $100 fine. By now, in his midforties, Woodley's challenge was to plow his little piece of land and grow as much cotton as he could—not to be perceived as sympathetic with the Reconstructionists and carpetbaggers who vowed to change the system. Woodley had more pressing problems. One of the antivagrancy laws required that by the second Monday in January 1866, all freedmen, free Negroes, and mulattoes in the state must produce written evidence proving they had a job and a place to live. Town officials had the power to arrest anyone violating the law, hold trials without juries for the suspects, and mete out sentences of ten days in jail and a $50 fine. If the convict didn't have any money, local sheriffs could give the violator back to his original master.

At some point, Woodley met and married a former slave named Kate. Not much is known about her or her family, except that she was raised by the white people, a not so subtle characterization of her working in the house as opposed to the field. The only story that Kate passed down was of the day her mother died. Kate was a little girl then, and her mother lay deathly sick in a back room. Their master, extremely protective of Kate and her mother, frantically paced back and forth near the room, occasionally going in to check on Kate's mother. Kate sat on the porch all day and watched the sun rise and eventually fall. As the sun fell, her master came from the back room. "She gone, little Katie, she gone," the master finally moaned.

Kate and Woodley Turnbull bore a son, Jake, in 1883. As best as we can tell, Jake eventually became a sharecropper like his daddy and worked the land. He had little education, maybe third grade, but could read and write well enough to get by. He married a woman named Francis Evans and they produced six children. The oldest one, Jake Jr., was my father. He was born in 1914, and by the time he turned thirteen, he had quit seventh grade and struck out on his own to become a man. He told everybody that he wanted to help his mama with his five younger brothers and sisters, but the truth of the matter was that he wanted to fool around and go hunting with his two older cousins. From then on, Jasse, as he was called, always hustled to have a little money in his pocket. He had a deep freezer that he kept filled with meat—coons, deer, rabbits, and squirrels. And fish. My daddy loved fishing, paddling his wooden boat out on rural creeks and sometimes the Mississippi River. He would string up his fishing pole, a long bamboo stick, and come back with tubs of fish.

I don't know when my father met my mother. But from what they tell me, it was love at first sight. My mother, Lena Green, was born and raised in Longswitch. She had an older sister, Sammie, a brother, Billy, and a half-brother, Booker. My mother's mother took Booker in and raised the children as if they were all brothers and sisters. It was only later in Booker's life that my grandmother told him that he shared only the same father with the other children in the house. Family members called my mother Bunche because, as the story went, she was as sweet as a bunch of flowers. Her parents died when she was small, and she moved to Greenville with her older sister, Sammie, to attend Coleman High, the colored school. She had become quite popular, and her striking looks melted Daddy. I'm not sure if they had a ceremony or not. I was born on July 19, 1944, in my aunt's house. Though thousands of blacks were riding the Illinois Central train past Longswitch to leave the Delta, my family stayed and depended on faith and a good education to deliver us to a Promised Land.

Childhood Memories

I REMEMBER THE day I lost my childhood. I was five years old, and mama was pregnant with my baby brother Horace. She had taken us to a Seventh Day Adventist Church revival, and after we returned that night, Daddy became furious at her decision to switch from the Baptist Church. I was sitting at the kitchen table with my sister, Mary, and my brother Sam. Daddy stomped around the table, hollering, until he went to the sink, turned on the faucet, and poured himself a glass of water. Mama remained pretty calm, but Daddy kept on fussing. He didn't hit her, but he eventually threw his water in her face. I didn't know what to do. I just began crying. Soon after that incident, she gathered her belongings and children and walked out the front door. Before we left, I saw my father loading some wood on the back of his pickup truck in our driveway.

"Daddy, Mama is leaving," I said.

"I don't care," he snapped.

We left the house on Delta and Hyman Streets and

moved in with my mother's sister, two blocks away, on Delta and Alexander Streets.

Part of me wanted to stay with my father. He had been decent, taking me out on his fishing trips and teaching me how to catch catfish and wide-mouth perches, some of which were as large as both of my father's hands held together. He was kind and gentle, and I can only remember him beating me once, probably for something that I deserved. Daddy left Greenville after a while and went to Chicago to join two of his brothers. He found work in a factory. After several months, he began coming back and forth to Greenville, picking up where he left off, working as a mechanic and running his struggling woodcutting business. My parents had a telephone conversation once in which I heard Mama talking about getting back together. But that never happened. My father wanted us to come to Chicago where he said life was better. I don't know if Mama wanted to go north or not. She decided to stay and endure on her own, and if she didn't have a man to share the load, she certainly had a son who would learn to pick up the slack. I learned quickly.

Mama was a tall woman. She played basketball on the team at Coleman High. Back in the mid-1930s, only the two best athletes on the team were allowed to run on both sides of the court. The other three players had to remain on one side or the other. She was one of the best athletes and during her senior year, made the All-State team. She graduated in 1936. She could read, write, and speak well. She had everything going for her, except her dark skin. Very few jobs existed for black high school graduates. For most of her life, she worked day and night, either cleaning or cooking for white folks. On a good week, she earned $20.

She considered herself blessed, nevertheless. Her older sister, Sammie Hollins, was the executor of their family properties. The Green family owned several acres of land in Longswitch and about half a block of land near the corner of Delta and Alexander, where Aunt Sammie lived, in the colored section of town. When Mama left Daddy, we stayed with Auntie for a while until she cleaned up a vacant house right on the corner of the family property. Our white clapboard home was larger than most of the shotgun houses that were built in the neighborhood. We had three bedrooms, a living room, a kitchen, and a side porch. We used an outhouse at first, and then eventually had a bathroom built near the kitchen. Each of us hung our clothes on nails. For bureaus we had what they called "shiffa-rows," which were wooden boxes that had a mirror on top and drawers inside. The three boys stayed in one bedroom; my sister, Mary, had one to herself. In our backyard, we had a chicken coop and a garden, where we grew peas, beans, watermelon, corn and greens, squash and tomatoes.

I never heard my mother complain about her life. For one thing, she never had time. She had to raise four children and work to makes ends meet. For another, she believed that the Lord would provide. She had faith, an unwavering sense of hope that the Lord would provide a better life, if not for her than at least for her children. "Just have faith," she would tell me. Her religious beliefs, however, did not cloud the reality of raising her children alone. She often told us about responsibility, how we had to help out around the house. "Faith without works is dead," she reminded us.

I took my mother's words very seriously and became her right hand. I was in charge of my younger brothers and sister in her absence and made sure the housework was done. I was very close to her. I felt her hurt whenever she cried. I felt her exhaustion when she came home from work and just sprawled out over her bed. She would be so tired—and would have to get up in the morning to start all over again. I remember her leaving in the morning when she worked as a domestic for a white family on the other side of Greenville. They would drive by and honk their horn to pick her up and drop her off later in the evening. When she didn't work as a domestic, she labored as a short-order cook at a motel. She worked the late shift, which in those days meant all night. For extra cash, she took in ironing for people and pressed women's hair.

Everyone in the neighborhood knew that she would do anything. It was once said that a mother's heart is a child's classroom. My mother had a big heart. Some might have taken advantage of her, but she never talked bad about them or said that she couldn't help them out because of something they did to her in the past. She just did it, and I modeled my life after hers. She didn't talk about what she had to do; she just worked until the job was done.

She was basically more spiritual than anything else. I think that is the reason that she was so calm: she prayed so much, asking the Lord for strength and endurance. She never lost her patience. One of our neighbors, Mrs. Hodges, had a troublemaker son named James who over the years has remained a close family friend. Mrs. Hodges was very protective of her James, who could do no wrong in her eyes. On one particular day, Mama was sitting on the porch. James had hit some kid and began running back home. The kid caught him and started beating him. Mrs. Hodges heard her son's screams and rushed out of her house, hollering at the boy who was atop her son, telling him to leave her son alone.

Mama calmly watched the whole incident. When Mrs. Hodges finished screaming, my mother called her over to the porch. "Mrs. Hodges, I saw the whole thing," Mama told her. "Your son James hit that little boy first. The little boy hit him back and your son started running and the boy chased him. I think if you start letting children be children, everything will be all right." Mrs. Hodges didn't like being reprimanded, but she still had the utmost respect for my mother. Everyone knew that she was for right and didn't care who that upset. Mama never had a negative tone in her voice. She was always calm. She told people when they were wrong, but never in a confrontational way. She always urged us to act like Christians, no matter what the circumstance. "Don't forget to pray," she reminded us constantly.

I did everything for her: mop floors, wash dishes, cook, clean. I helped wash clothes in our backyard by boiling water and pouring it into a large tub. I scrubbed the clothes on a ripple board with lye soap. I dressed my brothers and even braided my sister's hair before she went to school. Her hair might not have looked the way Mama would have done it, but it was the best that I could do. I made sure that they didn't burn themselves on the wood-burning stove. I was always fixing up the house. We were very poor, but I would go out in the garden and chop all the weeds down with a hoe. I wanted it to be the nicest on the block. Whenever I went outside the neighborhood to earn extra money by cutting grass, I would pull up patches of Bermuda grass, carry it home, and plant it in our yard. I trimmed our lawn and shrubs to keep everything neat. I saw how hard my mother worked, trying to make things right for us, and I did anything to make her life easier. Much has been said about mothers raising their children alone, a difficult task regardless of wealth. For me, life was very much about doing what needed to be done. I didn't have time to run around on the streets and hang out with my friends. My life was about work and responsibilities. I didn't want anyone to think that we were less-than, simply because my father was not around.

My neighborhood bred that sense of responsibility. Alexander Street was one of the main roads that traveled north to south through Greenville. Delta Street was a narrow gravel road back then. Everyone in the neighborhood acted as if they were all one family, which created a nurturing atmosphere for children. One of the advantages of segregation was that we could develop a sense of self-worth without the daily insults and put-downs. Everybody worked, and all of the families banded together to watch out for the children. It was one of those kinds of neighborhoods where neighbors had the full support of parents to whack their children on the tails if they acted up. The neighbors did more than just discipline; they also encouraged, always telling us to stay in school. We saw examples of hard work. Two doctors lived within a block, as did several business owners and educators. All of them wanted the next generation to have a better life than they had, and they knew education was the path. "You go on and get your education, sugar," one neighbor always told me. "You can be somebody. Keep on going to school." They were also fun. One of our favorite things was to play marching band, and the adults would laugh as we strutted along. I was always the drum major and used a stick or broom as my baton. All the neighborhood kids would get together and "play instruments," including a washtub serving as the drum.

Two elderly sisters, Miss Sue and Miss Essie, lived in a

shotgun house farther down Delta Street. Though my grandmother lived only five blocks away, they acted as if they were my grandparents, too. The Jackson family lived across the street. The father had what the neighbors called a "good job" in the post office and his wife, Millicent Jackson, taught children at the O'Bannon, the colored elementary school near Glen Allan, a small rural town about ten miles south of Greenville. She taught the sons and daughter of sharecroppers, many of whose education was interrupted by the rhythms of the cotton-picking seasons. The Jacksons had four children, and one would later become the first person I knew to attend college. The oldest daughter, whom I had a boyhood crush on, attended Fisk University in Nashville, Tennessee. The youngest son went on to become a doctor. Mrs. Jackson was always very proud of us. She was very nurturing and encouraging, always referring to me as Walter Jake, the same way Mama called me. A white family also lived in the neighborhood for a while. The Allens were pretty nice and they had a son named Sammy. For the most part, they got along with everyone along Delta Street, despite the social pressures from other whites. They were considered low-class: the father worked on a nearby plantation as a field hand and lived in the colored section. Even though the races were separated in schools and public transportation, poor whites and blacks worked together in low-end jobs and met at filling stations and neighborhood stores.

Sammy was a pretty nice kid until he called my younger brother Horace and a few of his friends "a bunch of niggers." All of them had walked to a corner store to buy some penny candy when a group of white teenagers pulled up. There was always tension when kids from different neighborhoods crossed paths, especially when different races were involved, but on this particular day, the tension escalated into ugly words. Whenever whites came around, black kids usually became quiet and suffered the nicks to their dignity with silence. Horace sensed trouble and started walking out the door. His black friends sensed the same thing and headed right behind Horace.

But Sammy froze for a moment, not knowing whether to stay, or leave with his black friends and risk being called a nigger lover. Sammy stayed, and as Horace and his buddies left, the white kids spat out insult after insult. Horace kept walking until he heard Sammy yell, "You bunch of niggers." Horace stopped for a moment and then kept on walking. It was one thing for a group of white strangers to say things, but not Sammy. We were growing up together, we played together. Horace never forgot those words. Nor did his friends. A few weeks later, they waited for Sammy to come outside and cross one of the overgrown fields near our house. Behind the tall grass and bushes, they beat Sammy pretty bad, but they still didn't feel any better.

The Allens later moved out and they were replaced by the Shanklins, a black family. We didn't know too much about them, except that Mr. Shanklin's nickname was Bubba. The Collinses lived next to the Shanklins. Mr. Collins owned a barbershop and his wife stayed at home. The Huddlestons lived next to the Collinses. He directed the Coleman High School band, considered one of the best in Mississippi. He also was a local musician, playing in blues clubs across the state. Around the corner, a few blocks down Alexander Street, was a grocery store, where we bought candy and cookies and other snacks. That store on Hyman Street was owned by a Chinese man. Another Chinese man owned a similiar store farther down Hyman Street.

On the south end of town was another colored neighborhood. It ran along Nelson Street and was better known for its juke joints, pool halls, bars, and liquor stores. As such, the neighborhood always attracted a seedier element, including pimps and prostitutes, drug dealers and winos. Back in the forties, the problem became serious enough that a group of black ministers pleaded with the city council to station a full-time police officer in the area. "We come tonight to bring to the attention of your honorable board the unsavory, unholy, indecent, uncivil, and all-but-unbearable behavior of the people in some of the colored districts of our city," the ministers wrote in a letter made public during the March 7, 1944, city council hearing. "In these districts a certain element of our people have broken all bonds of restraint, drinking, cursing, swearing, using all kinds of profanity in the presence of anybody and to anybody, boisterously blocking the street, fighting and displaying knives, and offering to fight otherwise peaceful pedestrians who must travel these streets for shopping, to get to and from churches, schools, and lodges. . . . And while everything bad—even killing—has already happened as a result of these unsavory conditions, if something be not done to prevent or restrain the people, this section of the city will be brought to an open shame and palpable disgrace. Such atrocities were never more rife in ancient Babylon, or in the slums of Chicago."

We spent most of our time at my aunt's house. Her name was Sammie Hollins, but when we were very small children, we couldn't really pronounce "Auntie." It came out "Nannie," and the name stuck. A field separated her white frame house from ours, and we would cut through the garden along the path leading to her back door. Nannie was a big woman and always had a little goodie in her apron to cure the skinned knee or hurt feelings. She helped Mama raise us. While my mother was quiet and introspective, Nannie was gregarious and lively. Mama had more education, but Nannie had more of a community presence. As my uncle Booker tells it, Nannie was very smart and was probably the best student of the family. But when their parents died, Nannie was left the responsibility of taking care of her younger siblings. Everybody knew Nannie. She ran a catering business and served some of the finest southern-style meals to the richest white people around. Though she was one of the few blacks registered to vote in the mid-1950s, she was not interested in politics as much as she was in business. She was always buying a piece of land here and there. She owned three lots in our neighborhood alone, as well as several acres of land in Longswitch. She was the family matriarch.

Nannie was a very loving person. She and Mama would meet in the field from time to time to catch up on things like two little girls. It was good to see my mother giggle with her big sister. Mama's parents had died when she was young, and Nannie, her older sister, took care of her. Nannie was best known for her cooking. Yes, Lord, she could cook. Everything. Steak and gravy, sweet-potato pie, biscuits. Anything you could name, she could cook well. Even those dainty little desserts that she served on her catering jobs. Whatever she was cooking for business, she left some for us and we would have a feast. For Christmas, we didn't have much in the way of toys. We usually received a new pair of pants or a new pair of shoes. But every year, Nannie would bake each of us our favorite cake. My favorite was coconut. Even though we weren't really well off, I thought we were.

Daddy would come around every now and then. He would drop off some fish he'd just caught or some venison. He rarely gave us any money, but he did what he could. As we got older, he would tell everybody that he sent his children to college. Now, we knew that he didn't put up much of anything, but he was proud and that is all that really mattered. Daddy loved us. We were excited whenever we saw him. We would run up and scream, "Hi, Daddy." He answered the same way every time. "Hey baaaby."

I never really connected with my father. I loved him, but there was nothing really to talk about. He got along better with Sam because Sam was interested in fixing cars and other mechanical things. I, too, could do all that stuff, like change the oil or clean the carburetor; I just hated all the grease and dirt that came along with working on cars. I never became excited, like Sam did, when Daddy told us to help him. My father probably didn't know what to do with me. I was more introspective, more creative. In some societies that was probably encouraged. But in the black families of the Deep South, it wasn't, and especially not by black fathers. Mothers understood and nurtured creativity. Mama was always encouraging me. Daddy was just there.

Becoming the best was a very difficult thing in Mississippi. The odds were so stacked against us, but as a child, I didn't know just how high. My first- and second-grade classes were held inside Greenville High School. It was run by the Pilgrim Rest Baptist Church, which was located on the south side of town near Nelson Street. Mama had been a member there before she became a Seventh Day Adventist. The Pilgrim Rest Baptist Church wanted to make inroads into the neighborhood where we lived and started the school. The name of the elementary school where I spent the next two years escapes me now, but it was later named after my fourth-grade teacher, Melissa Manning. The public school had about twenty classrooms. As far as I knew, we had everything that all elementary school children had: teachers, a blackboard, chairs, and desks.

Mrs. Gardner was my third-grade teacher, and I worked very hard, learning my spelling and math lessons. She taught us about hygiene and required her students to bring in a washcloth, a bar of soap, and a toothbrush from home. If she thought someone needed to use them, she would ask the child to go to the bathroom with his washcloth and other essentials. It was very embarrassing, but it worked. Our belongings were placed in a display case with our names attached to them and served as a constant reminder to respect ourselves and our classmates and teachers.

Mrs. Manning, who had taught my mother, was my fourth-grade teacher. She was very strict, and I had little choice but to work hard in her class. She hung the multiplication tables across the walls of her classroom. In order to pass her grade at the end of the year, every student had to know those tables. Mrs. Manning was perhaps the most influential teacher whom I had in elementary school. She was a real stickler for those tables, and I knew every one of them. All of the teachers were very encouraging, caring people who wanted us to be successful.

Life within the black community had its ups and down, but meetings of the races frequently resulted in unheard screams during the Mississippi night. I was ten years old when a group of white men murdered Emmett Till in August 1955. I didn't know him, but he was black like me, and his death made me realize just how precarious life was.

We had heard stories about lynchings and how black men were dragged through the streets, their feet strung to rear bumpers. The message was clear: stay in your place. Those stories were usually whispered by the adults, many of whom wanted us to believe in the goodness of humanity. I was never taught to hate white people. With the exception of Sammy Allen and his family, I never knew any. They lived on one side, and we lived on another. Schools were segregated, and so were the churches. Even the most liberal and prominent Greenville resident, William Alexander Percy, believed that blacks were "simple and affectionate." The wealthy cotton planter and poet typified the paternal-istic racism ingrained in many liberal hearts. After the 1927 flood, for instance, when the city was placed in a state of emergency requiring at least sixty thousand people, the majority black, to seek temporary housing, Percy headed up the relief efforts. He would later write, "Of course, none of us was influenced by what the Negroes themselves wanted: they had no capacity to plan for their own welfare; planning for them was another of our burdens." That was the reality, and no one really questioned the separation of the races when I was growing up. Emmett Till changed all of that.

As the story goes, the fourteen-year-old boy came down from Chicago to visit his relatives in Money, Mississippi, and supposedly whistled at a white woman in August 1955. He was shot in the head and thrown in the river with a cotton gin fan tied around his neck. In some versions of the story, he was found with his cut-off penis stuffed in his mouth. His mother wanted his remains shipped back to Chicago. *Jet* magazine, the weekly Bible of the black community, ran a photograph of Till lying in an open casket. The caption read: "Mutilated face of victim was left unretouched by mortician at mother's request. She said she wanted 'all the world' to witness the atrocity."

I had nightmares after I learned about the killing. As a child, I knew how to stay in my place. It was a matter of survival. Looking at a white woman was one of the first taboos. I still felt robbed, cheated of an innocence that life in America promised. Till's death caused the feelings once heard around the wood stoves to become full-fledged speeches in public view. Dr. T. R. M. Howard, a civil rights leader, was quoted in one newspaper as saying that if Till were a Mississippi farm boy instead of a Chicago lad on vacation in Mississippi, the world probably would never have known about his fate. "If all the rivers and swamps and woodlands of the southern countryside could recount the tales of the tens of thousands of Negro bodies thrust into watery graves, strung up on unoffending trees, tortured and murdered by church-going, Democratic-voting defenders of the 'American way of life,' their story would be too horrible for decent humanity to bear," he said.

The black church was probably the first support group. I don't recall Daddy ever going to church with us. He found inspiration in the bottom of a liquor bottle. I knew he wanted his children to grow up in the church. But I never quite understood his agitation when Mama switched from the Baptist Church to the Seventh Day Adventist. I'm sure he believed in God, but he rarely acted as if he did. Not like Mama. She took us to church every Sunday. That routine changed when we became Seventh Day Adventists. Church was on Saturday, and our Sabbath was from sundown Friday until sundown Saturday. Prayer services were on Wednesday night. The church was on the south side of town, about five miles away, and we either walked or caught a ride with someone who happened to be going that way. Mama's decision to join the Seventh Day Adventists caused a bit of a stir, and we were considered fanatics. We didn't eat pork. We didn't watch the high school football games on Friday nights. We didn't believe in premarital sex. I remembered when Mama told us that we were going to start going to a Seventh Day Adventist Church. There wasn't a discussion or anything; that's just the way it was. In a struggling black family, there were certain things that were beyond questioning. I guess I was just an obedient child.

I never really asked her anything about religion. I had to figure things out on my own. My understanding of God was limited, and based on the fire-and-brimstone sermons that I heard, I was afraid of God and interpreted biblical passages such as "God is a jealous God" literally. There was no question in my mind that God existed. I knew he was there, watching, and if you were a faithful person, he would reward you with eternal life in heaven on the glorious day when Jesus returned. But you would burn in hell if you were an unrepentant sinner. There was Good and Evil, nothing in between. Salvation was by his grace alone. No amount of obedience or money or works of charity could replace having faith in the Resurrection of Jesus Christ. I wanted to please God and be a good Christian, one of the chosen few. Like Jesus says in the Bible, "If ye love me, keep my commandments."

I couldn't wait for my baptism. I must have been twelve years old when I stood next to the baptism pool inside the church. "He that believeth and is baptized shall be saved," the pastor said. I remember stepping into the pool, wearing my blue jeans and shirt, and turning my back to the pastor and the congregation. I looked for my mother but couldn't find her among the proud faces in the packed sanctuary. I knew she was there, and I closed my eyes and waited for the pastor to lower me into the pool. I heard the congregation singing, "Take me to the water . . . to be baptized." I hit the cold water in a few seconds, stayed under for a moment, and stood up, as alive as the day I was born. I was soaked from head to toe, but my spirit was cleansed and energized. The congregation was now singing, "Nothing but the blood of Jesus" and "wash me as white as snow." It felt good.

I loved reading the Bible. I was always in Bible contests that tested knowledge of biblical facts and passages. I also loved Bible classes at school. The Bible was a textbook, and while we were only in a one-room schoolhouse, very important values were being instilled every day. So much of my foundation was learned then. My spirituality gave me a sense of faith and hope, and more important, influenced the way I conduct myself and view the conduct of others. In my mind, anything less than an A in Bible class was shameful. I especially remember the Parables. I read the Bible so much when I was young that it is integral to my life now and is a part of my everyday thinking. I don't know if I have one single favorite passage in the Bible, but the one that sticks with me is the Parable of the Talents. As the Parable goes, three people were given a talent. One multiplied his, another hid his under a bush, and another gave his away. I use that passage a lot at the boy's choir. I'm constantly telling the children that if they don't use their God-given gifts, he will take them away and give them to someone else. Most listen and work hard to develop whatever the Lord has blessed them with. Not all of the children can perform onstage or have a solo part. But I tell them that everyone is still born with ability. The question is how much they want to work to develop their skills. One of the lessons from the Parable of the Talents is that the one child who had less talent than another worked harder and accomplished more.

I learned about God's love in later years. I understand now that God is not just about punishment. I became more appreciative of God and began to understand man's proclivity toward sin and God's forgiveness. There is always hope, always forgiveness, always a chance for redemption by his grace. Throughout my life, I have had an abiding faith that God would provide, regardless of what people have said about me or done to me.

I had a lot of joy in my life growing up. Being a part of the church community and participating in church activities was fun and gave me a sense of belonging. The church was also the first place that I began to sing in front of people. That started when I joined the church choir. Singing came naturally to me. I had a beautiful soprano voice. It was lyrical, very pleasing. I remember praying to God that my voice would not change. People loved to hear me sing. Church ladies would come up to my mama, big smiles on their faces, praising my voice: "Your boy can sing, Sister Turnbull." Their compliments never went to my head. I loved singing for them. Probably, it was their reaction: they seemed to receive so much joy from listening to my voice. Sometimes I had a solo in church. People would come to me afterward and tell me how God had truly blessed me. All of that reaction was reinforcement and encouragement.

No matter how much joy I found in the church, work always interrupted. The housework was constant, and staying on top of my younger brothers and sisters became increasingly more difficult as they grew older and questioned my authority. Horace was the worst. Not only did he not want to do what he was supposed to do, he ran around the house, calling me names and then dashing out. His teasing was merciless. He said that I had "big bubble lips," and a lot worse. If I caught him, I tried to knock some sense into his head. I was fast in those days, and strong. Horace learned that after I caught him a few times. Horace must have vowed to himself after those beatings that he would never get caught again, because he surely ran whenever he said anything. He would get on my nerves so bad. Mary and Sam acted as the peacemakers. They understood that if Mama got home and the house wasn't cleaned, everybody would get in trouble. But sometimes, both of them would gang up against me.

To help Mama out, I worked in the cotton fields during the summer. I hated chopping cotton but would tolerate using a hoe and ridding the tall grass and weeds from around the cotton plants. The work was from sunup to sundown, or as the old-timers called it, from c'ain to c'aint. "C'ain" came each morning when it got light enough to see a hoe hit the ground before it hit your foot; "c'aint" arrived in the evening when it got too dark to hoe without chopping up the cotton. I had to wake up at 5 A.M. and walk down to the corner grocery store on Alexander and Hyman Streets. There was always a group of men and women standing outside the store, waiting for the pickup trucks to come by. The drivers of those trucks received money from the plantation owners depending on how many workers they brought. Sometimes our pay came from them; other times the owner would line us up, peel a couple of dollars from a wad of cash, and hand them to us at the end of the day. The scene at the corner grocery store rarely changed.

"Where ya'll going," someone would ask a driver.

"We're going out here to Longswitch to Mr. Smith's plantation," the driver answered.

"How much you payin'?" someone would ask.

"Three dollars," the driver said.

"How bad is it?" another person would ask.

"Ain't bad," the driver would say.

Now, if the driver said the plantation was paying $5 a day, rest assured that the grass was tall—and that the pickup truck would be very crowded. The work was plenty hard. Chopping cotton lasted throughout the summer, and on some occasions, if the cotton plants had matured enough before school began, I would be forced to pick cotton. I was never good at it. Picking the bolls of cotton from the plant strained the back and callused the hands. The plants were anywhere from knee-high to waist-high, which meant that either way you were stooped over. The bolls themselves were attached to a thorny stem, which ripped and scratched your unprotected hands. You were given a sack and expected to pick as much as possible. That meant the sack got heavier the more tired you became nearer the end of the day. Workers were paid by the hundred—$5 for every hundred pounds. Those who could pick two hundred pounds in a day were revered by the plantation owners, much like prize-fighters of the day.

Entire families would be out in the fields, young and old. The only thing that mattered was whether they were able to "make a day," which basically meant they could work the entire day without holding up the rest of the workers. Cotton plants were aligned in rows, and pickers worked from one side to the other, working until they started "pulling something"—a good load of cotton. If you were slow or weak, you were left behind. Some of the younger children served water to the workers. They sat near buckets filled with ice and carried a dipper with them. When workers became thirsty, the water boys lugged the bucket to the rows. Most of the workers carried their own cup. Sometimes they forgot and clasped their hands together. Most people brought their lunch and sat under a shade tree. A few went with the pickup truck drivers to a nearby store. Lunch was thirty minutes, sometimes an hour. There was no bathroom. It seemed like the last four hours were the hardest.

Chopping cotton was considered good work for us during the summer. When my brothers and sister and I could work the fields, we brought in an extra $12 a day to help Mama. I was still glad when school opened in the fall. I promised myself that I would excel in my studies because I had a dream: I did not want to chop cotton for the rest of my life.

Me and Miss Jones

THE STATE OF Mississippi and its people had a different career path for me. In fact, from the day I was born in 1944 to the day I left in 1966, Mississippi defied the U.S. Constitution by passing state laws and winking at social mores that kept blacks poor, powerless, and undereducated. When faced with the choice of economic advancement for all or preserving the racial status quo, they chose to spite their own fates and keep "the colored" in their place. I was guilty of one of the worst crimes—having an ambition. The segregationist logic was clear: economic equality led to political equality; both produced social equality, which in turn led to miscegenation. Segregation was about white purity and forced blacks to be deferential to whites in all matters. It meant addressing whites as "sir" and "ma'm," yielding on sidewalks, and never, ever looking directly at a white woman without risking an arrest for at least "reckless eyeballing" or worse, becoming, as Billie

Holiday sang, "strange fruit hanging from the poplar trees."

Even laws with noble intentions posed serious problems for the black community. For instance, the Greenville City Council passed an ordinance on November 6, 1951, outlawing ownership of "lower animals" within city limits. With the stroke of a pen, they thought that they could rid the city of nagging problems with public health. At the time, we had at least two cows, several hogs, and scores of chickens, ducks, and turkeys on our property. We suddenly became vegetarians long before that diet became fashionable. Our garden was well equipped to compensate for the loss of meat. We grew corn, okra, peas, squash, and butter beans. But I missed meat and, more important, the annual neighborhood gatherings in which the adults slaughtered a few animals in preparation for the winter. Those were big events in my neighborhood. Sometimes the men would go out hunting and bring back deer, racoons, rabbit, and all sorts of fowl. Other times they would kill one of their own cows or a few of their hogs. Either way, they gave each of the neighbors meat to last until spring. Most of the animal was used for something or other. For example, fat from the pig was thrown inside a black kettle filled with boiling water to make lye soap. Unless we went out to the country, those events were gone.

Instead of being able to produce all of our own food, at some point we began depending on what were called "commodities." Those products were government surplus flour, cheese, and butter. They also gave away canned meat, but the meat was pork, which was forbidden by the Seventh Day Adventists. Mama would trade her cans of meat for more flour or cheese. There were many nights when all we had to eat were biscuits. I could make them in my sleep. During the spring and summer, we would pick berries, pears, figs, apples, and peaches. Mama would can them for the winter. Those preserves spread across several biscuits served as dinner once in a while, and breakfast many mornings. My mother's brother, Uncle Billy, liked to joke about his biscuits: "Mine are so light, you can sweep the crumbs off the ceiling."

We never really had all the material things, and the loss of livestock was just another blow. Mama tried to instill in each of us a sense of optimism, a sense of hope. She taught us to always think positive, no matter what the obstacles. I saw how degraded black people were in Greenville. My desire to be somebody required transcending extremely difficult barriers. But I always did what I had to do. From an early age, I was very conscientious. I took my classes very seriously and made sure that my responsibilities at home were always taken care of. Mama tried to reward me as best she could. When I was ten years old, Mama gave me a Western Flier bicycle for Christmas. It was black and it had a little red-and-white piece of metal on the bar between the handlebars and seat. The bike was great and I rode it everywhere. Mama didn't have enough money to get Horace and Sam bikes. They improvised and made their own. They went to the junkyard and pieced together what they called "hot rods" from discarded scraps of metal. Their bikes had no fenders or brakes, and quite naturally they often came home with all sorts of scrapes and bruises.

There were some things that blacks could not improvise, though. Everything was all right as long as we stayed on our side of town. To make sure we understood our place, the Greenville City Council voted unanimously on June 6, 1944, to have a sign erected in the nearby Greenway Park

FOR WHITES ONLY. At the slightest inkling of blacks exercising any sign of independence, the white reaction was quick and decisive. The two decades of defiance by the state probably began shortly after the end of World War II. Thousands of blacks fought in that war, and those that survived came back only to face "colored" bathrooms and "white only" parks. Many of them, like my uncle Billy, headed straight to Detroit or Chicago to find work and a better place to live. Whenever he returned, we had a celebration. We would gather around and everyone would make a fuss about him. He would tell stories about the North and all of its glittering promise.

Their exodus had little bearing on local politicians. Sensing a newfound political independence by a few blacks, white politicians prepared for the potential of new black voters. Governor Fielding L. Wright called a special session of the state legislature in 1947 to strengthen Mississippi defenses by adding new voter laws. The U.S. Supreme Court outlawed "white primaries" in 1944, but legislators felt it necessary to protect "their" ballot box by empowering county election officials to challenge voters. To make sure the election officials knew whom to challenge, the lawmakers added, "Any person who has participated in three primary elections . . . shall not be subject to challenge."

Not that they really needed any new laws to stir up feelings of white superiority. U.S. Senator Theodore Bilbo already had done that with his blatant use of racial politics. During his campaign for a third term in the Senate, he called upon whites to use "any means" to keep Negroes from the polls. In case anyone needed clarification, he spelled it out during one of his campaign speeches: "I am calling upon every red-blooded American who believes in the superiority and integrity of the white race to get out and see that no nigger votes . . . and the best time to do it is the night before." Bilbo's deep-seated belief that blacks were inferior to whites was unrivaled in American history and helped foster the tension between whites and blacks when I was growing up. "They are only one hundred fifty years removed from Africa, where it was a great delight to cut him up some fried nigger steak for breakfast," Bilbo once said. He died, ironically, from cancer of the mouth in 1947 and never gained his third term as senator or completely answered charges that he received bribes from government contractors. His book, *Take Your Choice: Separation or Mongrelization*, survived, as did the reality of "separate but equal."

Back then, some were more equal than others. Of all the city employees, according to the minutes of the January 3, 1944, city council meeting, Julia Glover, "the colored librarian at the Colored Library," earned the least amount of money—$50 per month. Amanda Worthington, the "librarian," earned $137.50 per month. Charles Gray, the city hall janitor, earned $108.33. "Equality" was also seen in per-pupil expenditures. In 1940, the amount for whites was $41.71; for blacks, $7.24. The length of the school year for white children, unburdened with field work during cotton-picking season, was 160 days; for blacks, 124 days. Annual teacher salaries were $776 for whites, $232 for blacks. Twelve years later, in 1952, little progress had been made in narrowing the gap. Per-pupil expenditure for whites was $117.43; for blacks, $35.27. Although only nine days separated the white school year from the colored and teacher salaries had increased dramatically, the disparity persisted, with whites earning $1,991 and blacks, $1,091.

Politics and racial equality were issues that only God

could fix, and I left those problems to him. There was nothing else that I could do. As Seventh Day Adventists, we were more concerned with being saved and receiving a quality education. Attending a church school was one way that we could further strengthen our spirituality while assuring that we would not be damned to hell by attending a public school with the sinners and nonbelievers. Our church did not have a steeple or a single pane of stained glass. We sat on wooden seats bought from a run-down theater and prayed in a room without a cross or a picture of Jesus. The "schoolhouse" where I entered fifth grade was in another room connected to the main church building. The classroom had a blackboard and not much else. We had the traditional school desks, the ones with the woodens armrests attached to the seats. Our teacher was usually the pastor's wife, and able to provide lessons to students from kindergarten to eighth grade at the same time. Multiplication tables and alphabet letters hung from the walls. The classroom was quiet and orderly. There might have been about twenty children in the room. The fourth graders worked on their particular lessons in one corner of the room, while the eighth graders worked in another. Most of the children were about the same age and academic level, and I still wonder how we learned in such an environment. But we did.

Music had begun to grab my heart. Mama knew a nice lady, Mrs. Chisholm, who lived across town and gave piano lessons for twenty-five cents. She became my first piano teacher. The lessons were basic, and I remember Mrs. Chisholm smacking my hand whenever I played a wrong note.

My next piano teacher was Ruth Crawford. We called her "Auntie Ruth," and she was a member of the church. The funny thing about her was that she had just learned how to play herself. The young people's choir at the church was another extracurricular activity. We rehearsed on Friday nights, maybe six or seven of us, but we did not sing such music as gospel or pop. These were not considered to be the proper forms of praise to the Lord. Our music was choral, hymns and anthems. It was very beautiful and moving when the congregation and the choir raised their voices. When I was in ninth grade, Mama rented a room to Miss Barbara Lee. She was a young teacher fresh out of college, and it was customary for new teachers to room with a local family while they worked their first jobs in a new town. She was like a member of the family. She monitored our work and behavior both in and out of school. She was the first person I knew who belonged to the Columbia Record Club. She had a phonograph in her room, and from time to time, I would hear *Rhapsody in Blue* or *An American in Paris.* We never listened to pop music on the radio, and she let me have all her classical recordings. I thought those selections would be all right and certainly not sinful.

Mrs. Williams was one of my favorite teachers and she stayed at the church school until I completed eighth grade. Her husband was the pastor of the church. He was very nice and was much more accessible than many of the other church ministers. He didn't seem to look down upon us. He became my mentor, teaching me how to do basic carpentry. Of course, I was free labor, but I didn't mind. He was a carpenter by trade, a preacher by calling, and was responsible for rebuilding the Seventh Day Adventist Church in Leland, a small town about eight miles east of Greenville. He taught me how to lay tiles and hardwood floors as well as hang shingles on a roof. Near the end of my eighth-grade year, Elder Williams and his wife took me to Oakwood College Academy in Huntsville, Alabama, to see if I could attend ninth grade there. Oakwood College Academy was one of the Seventh Day Adventist schools, and many blacks Adventists received their high school education there. I have forgotten how much the tuition was, but I know we didn't have it. Elder Williams thought that if we went down to the school, he could help secure a part-time job for me and thus relieve the financial burden from Mama's tired shoulders. When we arrived, I noticed the sprawling lawns and tall pine trees. The campus was so large I thought that I would get lost just walking around. I was impressed and could barely contain my excitement about the possibility of actually learning at such a lovely place. I *had* to get a job. After talking with admission officers, Elder Williams and I went to the school's laundry. We talked with the supervisor and, praise the Lord, he promised a job.

Chopping cotton didn't seem to be as bad that summer. The calluses on my hands were soothed by the promise of pleasing God and learning among the saved. Time moved quickly, and when the day approached to register for school, I received bad news: another student got the laundry job. I was devastated. My family didn't have any money to pay for my education, and I had no alternative but to attend public school at Coleman High in Greenville. I was very hurt, but I knew I had to make the best of every situation. My mother reminded me that I could be a good Christian anywhere. It was hard trying to simply pick up and go on after having my dreams dashed in such a profound way. I was just so disappointed.

Shortly before Coleman High began classes, Sister Seard invited me and my brothers and sister to her house for Sabbath dinner one Saturday afternoon, as she often did. We played with her children, even though many of them thought they were better than us. Their father, who owned a company that specialized in moving houses from one location to another, filled in as pastor when Elder Williams was out of town. Their snobbery went beyond material things. The Seards tried to control the politics, business, and people of the church. Of course, Mr. Seard donated greatly to the Regional Adventists Conference, and that gave him a considerable amount of clout over the choice of new ministers and where money was spent. Adding to my discomfort was the fact that all the Seard children attended Oakwood. I certainly had the feeling that the Seards were being nice when they invited us over. Sister Seard enjoyed hearing me sing. She asked me if I had planned to join the glee club at Coleman. She told me that it was known throughout the state. I didn't know how to answer. I had never heard about the glee club, but Mrs. Seard's question piqued my interest because I loved singing. I told her that I would certainly try out.

Coleman High was about a mile from my house, down Alexander Street and right off Highway 1. It was named after Lizzie W. Coleman, the former principal of Elementary School No. 2. She worked there for forty years, teaching the sons and daughters of sharecroppers the basics and frequently urging them to "burn the midnight oil" and "be prepared." She never graduated from college, and she knew that preparation was one of the keys to survival. She improvised a work space under a stairwell to teach young men and women basic typewriting skills. She insisted that her teachers attend summer school and pass the state teachers examination. Her forte was mathematics, but her passion was literature. Her ability to memorize and recite long passages of poetry is still legendary. In the 1920s, when the Harlem Renaissance was starting to gain a foothold in

American culture, Coleman gave a series of lectures on Langston Hughes, Countee Cullen, and Claude McKay. The school board named the small brick high school in her honor in 1923.

My father's cousin, Matthew Page, graduated from Coleman in 1948. During his senior year, he learned chemistry and biology in the school's so-called science lab—a broom closet. Page and other students had a few test tubes and a minimum of other hand-me-down equipment from the white high school. Some of it was usable but most was too old to conduct the most basic of experiments. Page and a few of his friends decided one day to stop complaining among themselves and carry their tattered equipment to the school superintendent's office. The superintendent agreed to see them and was as pleasant as he could be to a group of young black teenagers. Page left the brief meeting thinking that something would be worked out. But as soon as the group returned to their classroom, an agitated Coleman High principal immediately suspended them for five days. Page went on to become a doctor, his success the result of sheer will, not his broom-closet education.

Coleman had grown since Page's days. The city council spent $400,000 in 1951 on improvements, including a full-fledged science lab. I started my ninth-grade classes in 1958, and I thought the school was really nice. It wasn't Oakwood College Academy, but for a "colored" school, it would have to do, and it was clear that state lawmakers were not going to change their views or spending on our schools. Four years earlier, the U.S. Supreme Court had handed down the *Brown* v. *Board of Education* decision outlawing segregation in the public schools. White Mississippians first reacted with shock, then concluded that there was little to fear because true believers in the "southern way of life" would neither tolerate nor obey the decision. To many, "all due deliberate speed" meant "not in my life-time." Others predicted violence. Fred Sullens, editor of the *Jackson Daily News* and the state's most widely read journalist, called the decision a "calamity" and expected bloodshed to follow: "Human blood may stain southern soil in many places because of this decision, but the dark red stains of the blood will be on the marble steps of the U.S. Supreme Court building." Sullens was not the only one to voice his opinion publicly. Tom Brady, a municipal judge from the small town of Brookhaven, gave a speech entitled "Black Monday" in which he stated: "We as Missis-sippians will not bow down to a court of nine old men whose hearts are as black as their robes. . . . We can die, if necessary, for our principles."

The black reaction was equally strong. On July 30, 1954, Dr. T. R. M. Howard delivered a speech before Governor Hugh White to discuss the "Negro's stand on segregation in its public schools":

> We realize that the Supreme Court has only said that segre-gation is unconstitutional. It has not said yet when and how it is to end. . . . You know, as well as we know, that we have had the *Separate* all right but in very few cases have we had the *Equal.* You have had a school equalization law here in Mississippi since 1890, but you forgot about this law until you began to feel the sharp lash of the Su-preme Court, and today you wish to bargain with us. . . .
>
> The Mississippi Negro public school system has been so lacking in buildings and facilities that the Negro children have developed a complex which has caused them to want to go to the white school in their community not because of social reasons but because the white school was the best

in the community. We believe that it is morally wrong for those who have sworn to uphold the laws of our land to talk about abolishing the public school system, in order to evade the laws of our land.

The public acrimony seemed so distant from my reality. I knew that I needed an education and that the only place I could learn was at Coleman. There were about six hundred other black students at the school. Within the first week, Herticene Jones, the glee club director, had paraded all of the new students into the music room and told us how fortunate we were to even have a glee club. She asked each of us to sing something. At her request, I sang "America, America." I knew the song by heart.

None of my high school teachers would have as profound an effect on me as Miss Jones. My biology teacher, Mr. Robert Young, came close, and in fact, I thought about majoring in biology in college to become a biology teacher as a result of his nurturing style of teaching. I also loved chemistry as taught by Mr. Long. I liked my English teacher, Mrs. Crawford. She always began her class, "You will do this assignment on . . ." But Miss Jones taught music and she instilled a desire to be the best. She knew that I had talent; she simply motivated me to work as hard as I could.

Miss Jones was a regal woman, grand in everything that she did. Born and raised in Greenville, she graduated from Coleman High in 1942 and went away to Alcorn State University. Her father, Oliver Jones, didn't want her to go to college, preferring instead for her to get a job, but she was determined to go anyway. She always said that she inherited her musical abilities from her mother. She began her formal music training when she was a child. She knew about hard work. She knew about discipline. She didn't care who liked her style or not. She was known to go on the football field and drag players from practice. Willie Richardson, who later would become a professional athlete, liked to walk the hall a lot. Miss Jones saw him one day and screamed, "Come in here, boy. You are in the choir." That stopped him from walking the halls and gave her a bass. She didn't care whether you could sing when you began. She could make bricks from straw, and voices from mumbles.

I don't know what I would have done had it not been for Miss Jones and music. I was known as a singer, much like others were known for their abilities to play basketball, and was very popular. For the most part, everyone respected one another. That is not to say that we didn't talk about each other. In fact, I was the butt of a lot of jokes. When I sang, I opened my mouth really wide, and everyone teased me about my big mouth. One of friends even drew a big mouth on a blackboard and wrote my name under it. Of course, they talked about my big lips, dark skin, and high butt. But no one begrudged talent. Everyone wanted to be the best and worked hard to achieve. I liked singing, so I spent a lot of my time in the choir room and studying music.

Few of my friends understood my absence from sports or hanging out. They were always talking about stolen bases or touchdowns and bragging about their abilities, both on the field and off. I loved football and could play with the best of them, but I knew that as a Seventh Day Adventist, sports were not in my future. Most of the high school games were played on Friday nights. That was during our Sabbath and out of the question. To keep our minds off worldly pleasures, the church held socials on Saturday night, where the "young people," about ten of us, could drink punch and play a variety of games. Card games like spades and poker were not allowed; those were considered sinful. Dancing was another forbidden excercise. Most of the families usually came, and the socials were a lot of fun. We played games like musical chairs and old maid and, on occasion, we went to the skating rink or bowling alley.

I received my first real lessons on life in eleventh grade. For one thing, Nannie had a stroke and died. Her death left all of us frazzled. It was the first time someone that close to us had passed away, and I was sad for a long time. It was a great loss. Nannie's death made my sister, Mary, get over one of her worst fears. She had always been afraid of the dead. When Nannie died, Mary walked into her house and looked at Nannie as she lay on her bed. Mary kissed her on the forehead and said good-bye. Mama, of course, knew Nannie was in heaven and would have none of the earthly worries that plagued those she left behind. Mama was also frazzled. Long considered the baby of the family, her membership in the Seventh Day Adventist Church caused relatives to shun her and us. When Nannie died, she became the executor of the estate and was required to take care of the family properties. She eventually sold the land between Nannie's and our house to the Hodges family. They quickly built a house on their land, and the well-worn path that connected us with Nannie was forever gone.

Mama decided to keep Nannie's old Chevrolet. It was black and had a manual shift on its column. Daddy came over to tune it up a little, and it ran pretty well. My brother Sam and I taught ourselves how to drive in that car. We would drive down Alexander Street from one stop sign to another, find a driveway to turn around, and drive back.

Sometimes we would go to the nearby filling station and put fifty cents worth of gasoline in the car. The car windows were either broken or gone, and on cold days, we would place flattened cardboard boxes in the window wells to keep the heat inside. We would take turns at the wheel, both of us getting a chance to work on our shifting and hand signals. Of course, Mama didn't know—and if she did, she never said anything about it to us.

I also began realizing that black was not beautiful. In some cases, black folks were more hung up on color than many whites. If you were light-skinned and had what they called "good" hair, then everyone assumed you were more intelligent and better-looking. Because I was dark-skinned and had strong African features, I often felt that I was not much to look at nor wanted. In a sense, it didn't really matter what whites thought because I was never around them. But the looks I received and the names I was called by other blacks stay with me to this day. I was good friends with a classmate named Marianne, who lived next door. She was very light, almost white. We were pretty close. Her mother, Mrs. Coleman, was a guidance counselor at Coleman High. At the time, I was taking piano lessons from Miss Jones at school and needed a piano to practice at night. Marianne had a piano, and I asked her mother if it would be all right if I practiced at her house. Marianne's grandmother was old and definitely color-struck. "I don't want my granddaughter playing with those niggers," she was once overheard saying. Marianne hated me for asking her mother to use her piano. But I did. I was determined to become a musician regardless of the cost.

I always had suspicions about the real reasons that Mrs. Coleman and another counselor, Mrs. Robinson, never encouraged me to go to college as they did my other friends.

They told me that I had an average IQ and that I should pursue a vocational career. That meant that I could not study trigonometry, physics, or calculus. I had to take geometry and chemistry and that was it. I had to choose either auto mechanics or brick masonry. I chose the latter because my father worked on cars and I hated the black grease. I chose the bricks. It was pretty strange to me, and I wasn't any good at it. I wanted to take the college prep course, like my classmates Robert "Muggy" Smith and Elmer Stovall. They were my friends, but I never felt close to them. I always felt that they thought they were better and smarter than me after the IQ episode. I believed that I was just as smart as they. I had a B+ average, and it seemed that I was denied the chance of taking college placement courses based on subjective reasons, rather than solely on my IQ test scores. Nonetheless, I assumed that I wasn't good or smart enough. The counselors encouraged my friends to go on to Tuskegee and other black colleges. Their IQs were lauded. I was told to learn a trade.

It didn't seem fair to me. I came home one day with my head down, my sensitivity unable to withstand the constant pricks to my self-esteem. Mama sat me down and talked with me about it. She told me that what people said didn't matter. The only thing that was important was doing what I wanted to do. She gave me courage to go on. If I believed in music before my counselors' evaluations, then I should quickly begin devoting all of my attention to becoming a musician—and I did. I set my sights on receiving a music scholarship. Back then, those were as important as athletic scholarships. Choirs could bring an institution prominence and money. Whenever any college recruiters came to Coleman and held auditions, I was determined to show them that I could sing. I also began spending more time with Leon "Dokey" Turner. He was a year younger than me, but we did a lot of our science projects together.

We all had our crosses to bear. Johnny Frazier was in eleventh grade and was one of the few people active in the NAACP. He wore suits and ties and spoke correct English. One day, he came to school wearing a placard: REMEMBER BROWN VERSUS BOARD OF EDUCATION. He walked through the halls and attended a few classes before he was called to the principal's office. His boldness had caused quite a stir. The fear of white retribution was so strong that many black adults simply didn't want any problems. It wasn't that they didn't want equal rights and opportunities. They just didn't want any trouble. The principal immediately suspended Johnny Frazier for a week. The Civil Rights movement was just percolating then in Mississippi during the late fifties. The White Citizens Council, however, had already launched their terror campaign to maintain segregation, and lots of black folks were quiet. Frazier was the first person that I saw stand up. We chuckled at his crazinesss like most teenagers do whenever someone stands up for something, but back then, standing up to white folks could get you killed. Everyone talked about Johnny Frazier for weeks, though. He served as a reminder that we were still inferior in white eyes.

I liked music but Miss Jones was tough. She would do anything for you, but she was not afraid to ridicule you or your family if you messed up. She didn't care who was around to hear either. If you came in late to a rehearsal, she embarrassed you. "I know you are not coming into my class late," she would snap. She was tall and dark-skinned and carried herself with a regal air. She was a member of the Alpha Kappa Alpha sorority, and she was not about fun and games. She was about perfection. Whatever she believed in, she was right. Even if she was wrong, she was right. She believed in hard work and discipline. Sometimes she had rehearsals from 6 to 10:30 at night, and she had a captive audience. At that time, the city didn't have McDonald's or Popeyes or other places where teenagers could find part-time jobs. She was keeping us off the streets and teaching us the value of hard work.

She had a lot of influence over our lives and used a combination of tools to motivate us. She kept a box of tissues atop her piano. If you were talkative and within arm's reach, rest assured she'd smack your head with the box. "Are you going to talk again?" she'd ask. "No ma'm, Miss Jones, no ma'm." She simply did not tolerate distractions. Or lack of concentration. If she heard someone singing a little off-key, she'd march over and stand in their face, saying, "Just what is that you are singing?" One time, the whole group was not singing to her satisfaction. She lined everyone up. "Okay, tenors over there, altos over there, and take your belts off," she ordered. She then asked each of us to sing our parts aloud, and if we messed up, we had to walk through the belt line, taking hits from the swinging belts. Nowadays, she would probably be sued for such behavior. But beating children was not her point. She wanted everyone to know that their part was vital to the whole. She knew that peer pressure could make children do the wrong thing. She simply flipped that notion on its head. The message was teamwork: everyone rises and falls with each individual voice. Public ridicule was another of her motivational tools. One time, she told all of us to march around the school building during the middle of the day, when everyone could see us, and rehearse our songs while doing the cakewalk.

Miss Jones was deeply religious and probably should

have been a counselor. If a student had any need, she dug into her own pocket and provided what she could. She had the ability to talk with a person and quickly figure out the true problems. She had a really good ear, not just for music but for people. She called students at home to ask if their parents needed anything. She invited people over to her home to read the Bible and pray. She believed in fairness for all, and was one of the most vocal members of an ad hoc teachers group fighting for equal pay. She almost lost her job after a meeting with the Greenville school committee and superintendent. They labeled her a "troublemaker" and characterized her efforts as "stirring up trouble." She never had a hate campaign against white people, but she believed that she was just as qualified to earn the same amount of pay as the white music teacher at Greenville High School. She didn't really participate in marches or rallies. She just fought in her own way. She helped organize most of the black music teachers across the state to make sure that their students received an education.

A lot of people were afraid of her, but she had a great sense of humor. As the story goes, the school superintendent needed some forms filled out by Miss Jones. He was afraid to deal with her directly so he dispatched an assistant.

"When can we expect to have the forms, Miss Jones?" the assistant asked.

"I don't know," Miss Jones told him. "The voice of the Lord has not spoken to me yet."

Startled, the assistant returned to the office to let his boss know that he had talked with her.

"Well, you go back and tell her that I have heard from the Lord," the superintendent said, "and he has told me that if those forms are not on my desk by Monday morning, Miss Jones won't have a job that afternoon.''

The assistant rushed back over to Coleman and told Miss Jones about his conversation with the superintendent. Miss Jones was quiet for a moment.

''I just heard the voice of the Lord,'' she said, ''and he says you will have your forms by Monday.''

Miss Jones had earned respect. For decades, she produced the best choir in the state. We won every statewide competition that we entered. When other choirs saw us in a festival, they knew that the best they could do was second place. I'm sure they worked hard, and they had some very talented singers. But we worked harder. The night before a competition, we had a rehearsal. Any wrong move we made, she would stop the rehearsal and complain. ''Do ya'll know how hard I work?'' she usually began. ''And you know I don't get any extra pay to come out here and spend time with ya'll. And for what? To listen to this? Is this all the gratitude I get? Some of your own parents don't care about you as much as I do, and this is what I get in return.'' A lot of times, she would just walk out the door, leaving us there to figure out what and how we had messed up. Later on, I figured out that she just wanted us to work a little harder. But at the time, we would rehearse for another hour or two just to get everything perfect. After we finished and felt that we were ready, we would call her up at home. Of course she would be half asleep and still complaining: ''Well, I don't think we're ready to go.''

''Miss Jones, Miss Jones,'' we usually begged over the telephone. ''We have worked everything out and could you come to school early tomorrow and we'll sing it for you. Can you come over at seven A.M.?''

"Well, all right," she would say, "and I'll see if we are ready."

We would tell everyone to be in the choir room at 6:45 A.M. and not to make a sound until Miss Jones arrived. She would come in and say, "I'm just going to sit here and listen. Somebody give 'em a pitch." And then we would sing and it would be good and she would smile. "You see?" she asked. "That extra little time that you put in really paid off. Now if you sing something like this, I think we can go and win this competition."

No other choir in the state could really touch us. We performed in churches in Greenville and other cities at local festivities and commencements. Our concerts attracted a mixed crowd, and we always received a standing ovation. People just couldn't help themselves. We traveled throughout the state, usually by bus. The sponsors of state competitions sent a list of music from which choirs selected their songs. The list usually included spirituals, classical music, and anthems. Miss Jones never selected the easy songs. She always picked the most difficult. And she always had us look a certain way. The girls wore gowns and the boys wore dark suits. She fretted over the scenery onstage. Everything had to be just so. That is just the way she was. She was a large lady, and she spent most of her money on pretty clothes. Everything was a production. I had a few solos and enjoyed enormous success as a singer. At a time when seemingly everyone told us how unworthy we were, Miss Jones taught us how to be proud, how to walk around the state of Mississippi with chests out and heads held high, never bowed.

Our high school graduation was grand. Our band, also the best in the state, played, and we sang maybe two or three songs. All the graduates sent out their graduation cards, and everybody in the neighborhood came. It was a proud event. Everyone was all smiles. It was an especially big day for me. Because of my voice, three colleges offered me full scholarships: Arkansas A&M, Mississippi Valley State, and Tougaloo College. Those were three more offers than any of my friends with high IQs received. I chose Tougaloo because it was the best academically. I thought that I would study music and become a music teacher and possibly conduct my own choir. But on graduation day, thoughts of my future were far away. I was so thankful that I had made it this far. I was finally going to college, with a full scholarship, and not heading where my guidance counselors thought: laying bricks or swinging a hoe.

Tougaloo

NANNIE'S OLD CHEVY carried me out of Greenville to the rich promise of a higher education. Daddy drove and I rode shotgun as we headed east along Route 82 through the rolling flat fields, then south, on Route 49, the two-lane roads winding past tiny dots on the Mississippi map, little towns such as Indianola, Belzoni, Anguilla, and Pocahontas. Daddy didn't say much during the two-hour drive, and I remained pretty quiet, too, just excited about going to school. Before I left, Mama had hugged me and reminded me to pray. She would eventually have four children attend and graduate from college. I was the first to leave home, though, and if she had any apprehensions, she hid them from me. Every now and then, as the car sped past the overflowing kudzu and hills near Yazoo City, I'd close my eyes and get lost in my imagination. Something usually jarred me back to reality, but for once, reality looked good from where I sat: the cottonfields were in the rearview mirror, and Tougaloo College was up ahead, shining like the

North Star, providing direction to my unbroken spirit, lyric tenor voice, and trunk filled with well-worn clothes.

My home for the next four years was tucked away in the middle of a dense forest of pines, massive hickories, and oaks adorned with Spanish moss. Indians had called the land "Tougaloo," meaning "at the fork of the stream." Before the Civil War, John Boddie had carved out two thousand acres of the land resting near the convergence of two streams and ran a plantation. Smitten with a young woman, Boddie built her a spacious antebellum mansion, complete with a cupola from which she could view the city of Jackson, the state capital, about seven miles away. But as the story goes, Boddie really built the cupola for himself in order to keep an eye on his slaves. Disgusted over the way he treated them, the woman supposedly left him. Boddie's financial ruin came after the Civil War, and opened the door for the American Missionary Association to buy five hundred acres of the moribund plantation for $10,500.

As time went on, the AMA would establish more than five hundred schools throughout the South, but from Tougaloo's very beginning in 1869, it sat on the other side of the Illinois Central railroad tracks. As the whispers went, Tougaloo was known initially as the place where the light-skinned children of masters and slaves attended school. Though those children were believed to be smarter and better-looking than those of darker complexion, the potential of all blacks to learn was an open question, largely because teaching former slaves how to read or write was a crime. Most whites were unaware of the faith blacks had in education and their determination to get it. Many whites thought educating blacks was a good idea, but integrating public institutions like the University of Mississippi in Oxford or allowing white women to become "nigger teachers" and work in colored-only schools was too loathsome to even consider.

The burden fell upon Christians and liberals scattered throughout the country. They came to Mississippi to teach students and train teachers. Their work at Tougaloo was slow. The curriculum consisted of both academics and industrial skills. To make up for the generations of poor or nonexistent schooling, Tougaloo opened a secondary school, starting from kindergarten. Fund-raising was abysmal. As at other struggling southern universities, school officials and teachers grew their own food and sold their own cotton. Most of the students found themselves working in the fields or cleaning the Mansion, which by then had become the main administrative building, to make ends meet. Tougaloo College awarded its first baccalaureate in 1901, thirty-two years after it opened. Booker T. Washington, a former slave and the founder of Tuskegee Institute, would have been proud. Six years earlier, Washington had proposed in a famous speech in Atlanta that blacks should set aside the goal of legal rights and concentrate instead on self-help, thus enabling the majority of poor, rural blacks to become economically self-sufficient without triggering white hostility.

As time passed, Tougaloo became better known as the one place in the state where blacks and whites actually lived, worked, and learned together. The twenty-five-foot high wrought-iron entrance gate, standing tall among the pine trees, marked a clear line. Inside the gates, as we called being on campus, meant safety, nurturing, support. Outside the gates meant the complete opposite: living in Mississippi. Tougaloo was an aberration, and a year before I drove through the gates in September 1962, Governor Ross

Barnett had already called the school "a cancer" within the state.

I didn't know much about Barnett, only what I gathered from newspapers and television reports. It seemed to me, based on his actions and stubborn rhetoric, that he was a typical segregationist. He was born in the hills of Standing Pine in 1898, and as a little boy, plowed fields and sawed wood for six cents an hour. He eventually became a lawyer, making about $100,000 a year. He never forgot his homey background, and when he became governor, job seekers formed a line in front of his office forty yards long. He defended his resistance to integration by arguing that "God was the original segregationist." He claimed to have black friends. To prove it, he told the story about how he had given one such friend, Dorsie Moore, a bird dog trainer, $1,100 because he liked him. Barnett probably honestly believed that he had black friends, and that was one of the things that always struck me about segregationists: as long as they had the power, it was all right for blacks and whites to be "friends."

By Barnett's definition, "cancer" was spreading throughout the country. Though the Civil Rights movement had taken hold in the Deep South, Mississippi was different. White resistance was organized and sanctioned by virtually every level of government. Shortly after the *Brown* v. *Board of Education* decision, the state legislature passed several laws aimed at reversing federal efforts at integration. The laws permitted the abolition of public schools, allowed tuition grants to students attending private schools, limited civil rights protests by curtailing First Amendment rights, and created the State Sovereignty Commission, an organization charged with protecting states' rights and preventing federal intervention.

Commission members took pride in the fact that the civil rights demonstrations taking place in other parts of the Deep South had not occurred in Mississippi. As long as they were around, they boasted, segregation would remain if not the law of the land then certainly the practice. The commission spent $5,000 a month to help fund the White Citizens Council, the shadowy statewide group that began in Indianola. Composed mostly of urban middle-class professional men, the council unified whites and ensured that blacks remained quiet and nonmilitant. The council renounced violence, at least publicly, and preferred instead to rely on economic pressure, political intimidation, social ostracism, and propaganda.

If those tactics failed, murder was always an alternative—and virtually free of immediate punishment. On September 25, 1961, according to statements given later to the U.S. Commission on Civil Rights, State Representative Eugene H. Hurst drove behind Herbert Lee as they pulled into a cotton gin in Liberty, Mississippi, a rural town near the Louisiana border. Lee, a farmer, had attended several voter registration meetings organized by the Student Non-Violent Coordinating Committee and had driven SNCC leaders around to meet other farmers in the political district. At the cotton gin, Hurst, a member of the White Citizens Council, got out of his car and began talking with Lee. All of a sudden, according to three witnesses, Hurst pulled out a gun. Lee scurried out of his pickup truck by opening the passenger-side door, but Hurst ran over to him and shot him once in the temple, dead.

A deputy sheriff later asked one of the witnesses, "Didn't you see the tire iron?" The witness told the sheriff that he had not seen one in Lee's hands. The sheriff insisted, "Well, there was one." The witness testified at a later coroner's hearing that there was a tire iron. Before the subsequent grand jury hearing, the witness talked with Bob Moses, an SNCC member, about the possibility of federal protection if he told the truth. Moses and other SNCC workers called the Department of Justice and were told that they could not make such a guarantee. To make matters worse, an FBI official told the deputy sheriff about the witness's willingness to tell the truth. The witness was immediately beaten and, quite naturally, lied to the grand jury. No charges were ever brought against Hurst, and two and a half years later, the witness was murdered by someone whose identity was never revealed.

Word about Lee's murder spread inside the gates. Medgar Evers investigated such murders as the field representative for the NAACP. He was the Civil Rights movement in Mississippi, stirring the racial pot in a state not listening. For years, he worked by himself, mostly from his home in Jackson. He spent part of his time examining mangled bodies and reporting back to NAACP headquarters in New York. Most of his time was spent trying to persuade the reluctant to stake their lives on a shaky bet called voting. The near certain punishment faced by blacks who spoke out or registered to vote was too difficult a choice, no matter the potential for change. The lives we had might have been bad, but "agitatin'" could cost even that. From the time Evers began working for the NAACP in 1954, he received little statewide support and was largely ignored by local media and state government agencies. We knew that our lives were filled with suffering, but at least we had hope. We firmly believed in God and good education to change the ways of society. Evers believed in those two institutions, too, but he added a third—protest.

He organized students at Tougaloo College. Robert Honeysucker, one of my friends and mentors and the star baritone in the Tougaloo Choir, was a freshman when he first met Evers in 1960. Honeysucker had been involved in voter registration drives as a high school senior in Memphis and was struck by how even-tempered Evers appeared. He was not negative or hateful but a person who could make a demand without being confrontational. He challenged students to care about their lives and society. Caring was the first step. The next, he urged, was to get involved by helping people to register to vote. He was convinced that the only way to force social change was not through violence but through the ballot box. "He was a very kind and gentle man," Honeysucker recalls. "And very much driven to generate a change in the way things were."

Nine Tougaloo students changed the way things were in March 1961, one year after the sit-ins in Greensboro, North Carolina. It was the first civil rights demonstration in the history of Mississippi. The Tougaloo Nine walked into the main library in Jackson, calmly asked for reference books and the card catalog, and were promptly arrested. "There's a colored library on Mill Street," the police told them. "You are welcome there." Two days later, when the students were tried on charges of refusing a policeman's order to disperse, the police prevented a crowd of blacks, including Evers, from attending the trial in the municipal courtroom by beating them with clubs and unleashing their German shepherds. During the subsequent hearings, student attorneys argued that the demonstrators had conducted themselves in an orderly manner. Judge James Spencer agreed with the lawyers but said the Negroes were guilty anyway. The judge ruled that even though their conduct was orderly, it could have touched off a breach of the peace by someone else. Despite the apparent setback, Evers had some good news to report back to NAACP Executive Secretary Roy Wilkins: "This act of bravery and concern on the part of these nine young people has seemed to electrify Negroes' desire for freedom here in Mississippi."

Tougaloo President Adam Beittel understood the shifting social fault lines and set the tone for the campus by defending integration and encouraging challenges to Mississippi's racist society. Beittel also allowed the college to host visiting groups, many of which had both blacks and whites as members. That policy was so controversial that the only white Mississippian on Tougaloo's board of trustees resigned in protest. Beittel, who was white, was not very popular outside of the campus. Several months after the Tougaloo library sit-in, he appeared on a Jackson televison station WLBT with a panel of local reporters. Their first question: "Are you a member of the NAACP?" Beitell answered that he was not a member but he read *Crisis*, the NAACP magazine.

The reporters hovered around the explosive issues surrounding the library protest by asking if he thought Tougaloo's library was inadequate. Beittel went right to the heart of the matter. "I don't think the students came to the Jackson library primarily for books," he told them. He explained that they felt the injustice of being refused use of a public facility and that they had the support of the Tougaloo faculty, administration, and board of trustees. Dr. Beitell said he had not been in on the planning of the sit-in but that as soon as he had learned students were in jail he got them out on bail. Asked if he would expel the students, Dr. Beittel answered, "There is a difference between going to jail for stealing something and going to jail for a conviction. I should respect the students for being willing to pay the price for what they believe to be right." Dr. Beitell was asked if he thought it right to oppose community customs and rules. He answered, "All customs and rules should be abided by when they are consistent with our highest ideals."

For the most part, our goal was to survive in a society everyone knew was unfair. The challenge was to remain focused, regardless of the political and social turmoil sweeping the state and nation. My mission was simple: I wanted to work hard and get a good job in order to help my mother. Not that she would ask for my help. She was an extremely proud woman and never accepted a handout. As poor as we were, I remember her sitting down at the kitchen table and telling me that she was not going to accept welfare. "We will make it on our own," she declared. Tougaloo had scores of students like me who were determined to make it. Doing well in school and remaining focused were encouraged at Tougaloo. Everyone knew that many students who wanted to be involved in the civil rights demonstrations couldn't for a variety of reasons. Repercussions could cost a job or life. Some of the parents were still sharecroppers, their lives totally dependent upon the plantation owners. Others had parents who were untenured schoolteachers or post office workers, capable of being fired without notice or cause.

I was the first in my family to attend college, and though that was quite an accomplishment in itself, Tougaloo represented something more to me. For the first time, I felt really accepted. That feeling gave me the foundation from which to explore my intellectual curiosity. It was an exciting time, and life inside the gates was wonderful. We had the usual worries: waking up for 8 A.M. classes, eating horrible cafeteria food, living in cramped rooms, and scurrying about on Sunday mornings to find a clean shirt and tie to wear to mandatory chapel services. About six hundred students attended Tougaloo when I was there. Teachers called us by our last names and used the appropriate honorific. In jest, some of them called me Mr. Bull because of my last name. With such a small student body, everyone knew everyone else. Very few students had cars, so everyone stayed on campus. My two roommates, Henry Armstrong and Lawrence Jordan, were also from Greenville, but their personalities couldn't have been more different. Armstrong was brilliant in math, and we had worked together on algebra and geometry in high school. We couldn't wait to go to college. L.J. on the other hand was a partyer, always staying up late at night, playing cards, and talking trash. He was smart but didn't do very much studying as far as I could see.

How anyone could go to Tougaloo at that particular time and not be motivated to study hard was beyond me. There were seminars and guest lecturers almost every week. Dr. Ernst Borinski, a nationally known sociologist, organized meetings to discuss and debate issues such as civil rights and integration which attracted white students and professors, mainly from nearby Millsaps College. Dr. Borinski headed the Social Science Forum. Bo-Bo, as we called him, was Jewish and had escaped Nazi Germany by emigrating to America. Bo-Bo, really cared about Tougaloo students and was responsible for getting well-known, often controversial speakers to give lectures. He led debates, usually attended by the local media, arguing that integration was the Christian thing to do. All the Negro wants, Borenski once said, is "to ride the bus in the seat he chooses, go to the schools which are the best, and go to the shows where the best movies are shown." Those kinds of statements landed Borinski in the newspapers and, worse, got him excoriated on the state house floor. One state representative told the *Clarion-Ledger*: "This white professor at a Negro college has been making some pretty brave statements." Both the Senate and the House would later vote unanimously to investigate the means, methods, and "ultimate objectives in this state" of the NAACP, and another state representative urged that Borenski be included in the investigation.

Newspaper stories depicted the school as a haven for communists, northern agitators, and heretics. For me, Tougaloo was the first place I ever interacted with whites as either teachers or fellow students. William Kunstler's daughter, Karen, was one of the white students. I would see her and other whites from time to time around campus. We were cordial and that was the extent of our relationship back then. Their whiteness was not particularly significant to me, one way or another. Integration was nothing new at Tougaloo, and everyone had a certain sense of independence and ability to talk freely. The Civil Rights movement was the total obsession of everybody around. We rushed to the library to read the latest news stories on the pronouncements of the White Citizens Council or Dr. Martin Luther King, Jr. Many of the freedom riders stayed on our campus, and virtually every civil rights leader, from Dr. Martin Luther King to Dick Gregory, from Fannie Lou Hamer to Roy Wilkins, visited, lectured, or organized. During the "Freedom Summer" of 1964, for instance, President Beittel allowed a march to end at Tougaloo and permitted a concert featuring Frank Sinatra, Sammy Davis Jr., Marlon Brando, Burt Lancaster, and Gregory Peck. Dr. King estimated at least twenty-five thousand people would show up.

Even though Tougaloo was branded as a "hotbed of civil

rights activity," we were spared frequent acts of retaliation. That is not to say they didn't try. There were at least three cross burnings outside the campus and numerous bullet holes found on nearby street signs and houses. They served as a reminder: our welcome extended as far as the gates. White legislators tried to cut our state funding, but those meager efforts paled in comparison to the riots they created at other college campuses. During my freshman year, James Meredith tried to enroll as a student at the University of Mississippi at Oxford. He needed twelve thousand federal troops. The ugly episode exposed the duplicitous behavior of Governor Barnett. As we later learned, he spent most of his time talking with Attorney General Robert Kennedy, trying to work out a face-saving deal. But at the time, he spat out defiance: "We must either submit to the unlawful dictates of the federal government, or stand up like men and tell them never," he roared. "Every public official, including myself, should be prepared to make the choice tonight whether he is willing to go to jail, if necesssary, to keep faith with people who have placed their welfare in his hands."

Unlike many institutions of higher learning, Tougaloo was nurturing. Many of us responded by working four times as hard. Involvement in the Civil Rights movement marches and protests was considered extracurricular; we still had to attend classes and graduate. I didn't participate in any of the marches or sit-ins, but my actions were not interpreted as apathetic or timid. When it came to the movement, everyone was on the same page. It touched us all. Most of the professors understood the times and our anger. Our teachers may have flunked us a couple of times, but no one allowed you to fail completely. For the most part, solutions were always found. Honeysucker told me about the time his history professor summoned him to her office one afternoon. He had chosen history as a major simply by looking at the course catalog and choosing the first subject that sounded somewhat interesting. By the end of his first semester, his history professor told him that she had concluded that he and history were not made for each other. "What do you think, Mr. Honeysucker?" "I don't really know," he told me he responded. "Well," she said. "I have taken the liberty of talking to the music director about changing your major to music." "When is that appointment?" Honeysucker asked. She looked at her watch and told him, "Right about now." The professor walked him over to the music building and changed his major that day.

The music building had become my center of attention by choice. Much like football players of today, choir members came to school about two weeks earlier than regular students and rehearsed every day, usually for three hours before lunch, three hours before dinner, and a couple more hours later at night. We had to prepare not only for road performances but also for the mandatory Sunday services. Rehearsals often included practices on Saturdays and Sundays. If Herticene Jones taught me the basics in high school, Tougaloo's choir director, Ariel Lovelace, gave me the polish. He was like a father to me; and while Miss Jones was more of a disciplinarian, Pops, as everyone called him, was more of a motivator. He treated everyone like an adult and stayed out of their business. He was one of the best conductors around, his work known throughout the Midwest, including big cities like Chicago and small towns like Waukesha, Wisconsin. He had control over scholarships and grades and therefore wielded a considerable amount of power and influence over students' lives. He wasn't dogmatic or threatening, but most knew that he was a perfectionist who didn't suffer fools patiently. He expected the best and commanded with a soft, even voice.

Pops seemed to know most of the high school choir directors in the South and Midwest. He graduated from the American Conservatory of Music and earned a master's from the Sherwood Music School. At one time or another, he had served as a choral director in the Dayton, Ohio, public schools, at Alabama State Teachers College, at Jackson State University, and at Arkansas A&M University. Herticene Jones knew him, as did Bobby Cooper, another high school choir director near Jackson. Cooper had graduated from Tougaloo and had little problem telling Pops to give three or four scholarships to his best students. Pops usually did so without much questioning. That changed when Pops auditioned Constance Slaughter, who would later become the first black to attend the University of Mississippi Law School and is now the assistant secretary of state of Mississippi. For whatever reason, Cooper had forgotten to tell Pops that Constance couldn't read music. Pops usually found everything out sooner or later anyway, but unfortunately for Constance, Pops made the startling discovery on her first day.

In high school, Constance had grown accustomed to Cooper giving her a key on a piano so that she could start singing. But Pops simply handed her the music and asked her to begin. Constance, bubbling with pride, patiently waited for someone to start playing the piano to start her off. The key was not coming and Constance stood there, music in her hands, silent. "What do I do?" Constance asked. "You read music, of course, don't you?" Pops asked. "No, but I can sing," Constance bragged. Everybody laughed. In his usual dry way, Pops gave her one of those I-don't-believe-this looks.

"He was really taken aback that I would even have the gall to show up in his classroom without knowing how to read music and try to sing," Constance said. "I was going to sing. Really, I would have sung the song well, but I just couldn't read the music." Pops called her over. He didn't have to tell her that her singing career was over; she knew automatically.

"I really didn't feel that bad," she said. "I knew in my heart that I wasn't that good. And I wasn't as gung ho about being in the choir. Bobby Cooper wanted me to be in it, but I was more interested in being pre-med."

There was a certain amount of prestige associated with being a member of the Tougaloo Choir. When the choir performed on campus at the Woodworth Chapel, people, mostly students, jammed into every nook and cranny. Pops performed world-class music. Whatever feeling or message the composer tried to convey, Pops's interpretation was always on the money. Pops was the consummate performer. Concerts were an experience. We had a rich sound and sang beautiful music by composers as diverse as Handel, Mozart, Ellington, and Ninos.

Pops was a classy, elegant man. The son of a preacher, the Reverend William Lovelace, he was born in Gary, Indiana, on January 17, 1908. Tall and slender, he wore a suit every day, rarely dressing down. He'd take off his jacket during rehearsals and use his handkerchief to wipe what little sweat he generated. He married Edna Redlind, believed to be one of the richest black women in Jackson, and called her Sweet Petunia. She drove a new Cadillac Fleetwood almost every year. Wild colors, too; light green one year, light blue the next. I remember the first time I met her. Pops had told me to leave rehearsal and tell Sweet Petunia that he would be out in a few minutes. I ran out to the lobby and asked the only woman I could find, "Excuse me, ma'm, are you Sweet Petunia?" She was. Every year, Pops would invite the choir to his house for Christmas. Their home was quaint, very neat. It wasn't located in the wealthiest part of Jackson, but the furniture was nice, and expensive art and African artifacts hung on the walls. They were comfortable, and money was no stranger there.

I can't remember all the things that Pops told me or did. But he was the kind of man who taught me a lot about life. In hindsight, he wasn't a great voice instructor, and I probably learned more about the voice in graduate school than I did under him. But I learned so much about other things that his weakness as a voice instructor paled in comparison. He taught me how to be a man of substance, a man of character, and yet be a man capable of showing his vulnerabilities. He allowed himself to be open, which even today for a black man is considered atypical at best and weak at worst. Pops did not try to hide under a veneer of toughness. He was tough, but he was also able to share his fears and weaknesses in a way that made him no less a man. As the stereotype went, black men couldn't show a vulnerable side, especially in the Deep South. If anything, blacks wanted to show a mental toughness, a certain level of racial pride and integrity.

Every summer, Pops went north to work as music director for the Ohio Farm Bureau Youth Schools and the Wisconsin University Recreation Program. He was treated with respect and dignity and in a sense was given a three-month reprieve from being a black man in the Deep South. I knew that Pops had a commitment to teaching and to helping us understand our responsibilities as people of color at that time. During one choir rehearsal, a student showed up late and explained that he had overslept. The explanation angered Pops. He quickly told the student that if he was ever late again in the future, lie to him. "Tell me anything happened, but don't tell me that you overslept," Pops thundered. "We have been sleeping too long already as a people, and you can't afford to oversleep." With that, Pops continued the rehearsal. But it told us that Pops was about the business of making sure that we became responsible members of society. The Civil Rights movement was one thing, but we couldn't expect anyone to accept us if we didn't even respect ourselves.

Pops made sure that we knew the social graces. Every year, he would bring a full place setting to choir rehearsal and teach each and every one of us how to eat from a formal dining table. He wasn't stuffy at all; he was able to talk with anyone, regardless of their station in life. The Tougaloo Choir toured the country, usually playing at places that were connected to the American Missionary Association churches or in cities with strong Tougaloo alumni associations, such as Detroit or Chicago. We played in a lot of towns that we had never heard of before: strange towns in Wisconsin, Minnesota, Ohio, and Iowa. The tours were the best experience for most of us because we had never seen any part of the country except Mississippi. We couldn't afford hotels and depended on local church members to put us up for the night. We once gave a concert on a dairy farm in Iowa. The barn had been converted into a church, and we were singing Mozart and Haydn before an all-white crowd. We didn't know what to think, but the audience knew when to applaud and appeared to thoroughly enjoy the show.

The tours also gave us another perspective on life.

Spending the night at different homes was always the subject of conversation the next morning on the bus. Pops never wanted to hear any of our stories and remained aloof. A common complaint was how cold our hosts kept their houses. Most of us were accustomed to at least eighty-degree heat, but seeing our breath before closing our eyes was simply different. The most common complaint was the food. We weren't unappreciative and fully understood that food reflected a certain culture. Ours definitely clashed. Some fared better than others, but very few of us ever quite understood the concept of a continental breakfast. Most of us came from good-size families and grew up eating large meals first thing in the morning: grits, eggs, bacon, pancakes, biscuits. But on the road, some of our hosts served only juice, pastry, and maybe some fruit. One student boldly asked: "Okay, now that I have had this fruit and doughnut, where is the rest of breakfast?"

Larry Robinson told a story about one morning in Providence, Rhode Island, at the home of a middle-class couple: he was a professor at Brown University, she a housewife. To make us feel comfortable, she had decided to go out to a grocery store and buy eggs, bacon, and grits. Of course, the store didn't have grits, so she bought cornmeal and boiled it for three minutes. It wasn't cooked long enough, but the eggs were even worse. She tried to scramble them, but she put some water in the skillet, cracked the eggs, and stirred it together. Robinson and his roommate, George Patrick, who stood six feet six and weighed about 250 pounds, tried to be polite for a while, but they couldn't control it for long. Robinson spoke up. "Ma'm, I don't mean to be offensive or anything, but we are not accustomed to this kind of food. Would you mind if I fixed breakfast?" Robinson found oatmeal in one of the cabinets and some wheat bread and fixed breakfast for everyone. Robinson waited until they arrived back on campus before telling Pops. "You're lying, Larry, you're lying," Pops said.

Pops had a way of allowing his students to figure things out on their own. We had performed in Flint, Michigan, one year and were getting back on the bus to head back to Tougaloo. Pops always sat in the front, across from the bus driver, and greeted each of us as we carried our belongings on board. He said, "Good morning" to one student who promptly responded, "What's so good about it?" The student had spent the night at a struggling opera singer's apartment. She had only one bed and he had to sleep on the floor. Pops was quick: "If you don't think this is a good morning, you can just get your stuff and get off this bus."

The student promptly gathered his stuff and left. Pops followed him. "What are you doing?" he asked. "You told me to get off the bus if I didn't think it was a good morning," the student answered. Pops had had enough: "Boy, I should kill you. What is your problem?" The student went on to explain what had happened the night before, and Pops seemingly understood. "Okay, you deserve to go." Now the student had a problem. He thought about it for a couple of minutes and told Pops that he wanted to apologize because he had the wrong attitude. That wasn't good enough for Pops. "You need to apologize to me on the bus," Pops said. "Your attitude was public so your apology should be public, too." The student swallowed his pride.

Like most college campuses, Tougaloo was divided into niches: choir members hung out with other singers, students involved with the Civil Rights movement hung out with their colleagues. Unlike the majority of the students, those involved with the movement, particularly the white students, dressed very funky—jeans, T-shirts, and sandals. Most of the other students dressed up, some wearing shirts and ties or dresses. By far the most dominant groups were the black fraternities and sororities. Tougaloo had Alpha Psi Alpha, Omega Psi Phi, Delta Sigma Theta, Alpha Kappa Alpha, Kappa Alpha Psi, and Zeta Phi Beta. I wanted to join the Alphas. Most of my friends were Alphas, and they were considered to be the smartest men on campus, the class-A acts. I hung out with them so much that people just knew that I was an Alpha. But I couldn't join a fraternity. It was considered against the policy of the Seventh Day Adventists. "It's not what God wants," church officials told me. I wrote letters to church officials at the local South Central Conference in Nashville, Tennessee, asking for their guidance. My letters were never answered. A few of the Alphas even wrote the church on my behalf. They, too, were ignored. I still wanted to please God, but I found the church stifling in some ways, forcing me to walk an unreasonable line. I never joined a frat, nor was I very happy with the church's lack of sensitivity. I guess being in the world and not of the world was the guiding principle.

I also found myself constantly balancing between the different factions on campus. For one thing, Pops had selected me as tenor soloist, a position unheard of for a freshman. I had beaten out Clarence Johnson, a very talented, respected, and popular upperclassman, during an audition for tenor soloists for the annual presentation of Handel's *Messiah*. That created a mild stir and triggered some tensions and jealousies within the choir. The situation was made tenable because no one really questioned Pops's tastes or selections. The competition between fraternities and sororities was also very real and went beyond the fraternity initiation rituals of marching and step shows. Each group wanted to be known as the best and most connected on campus, lobbying hard for its members to be elected to student government and other coveted positions. I was also a resident assistant, forced to deal with the usual problems that students encountered living with each other— roommate disputes, loud noises, and sneaking alcohol into the building. Nonetheless, life in the dormitory was a lot of fun because there was always something or someone to laugh about. We joked about each other's peculiarities, grooming practices, clothing, and mannerisms. We would sit around and imitate each other. My friends loved to talk about my self-righteousness.

The Civil Rights movement created one of the sharpest splits among students. Some courageously believed in non-violence, attending seminars where their instructors cursed and slapped and spit on them to make sure they didn't raise their fists in return during a demonstration. The training served them well. On May 28, 1962, a group of Tougaloo students, including Anne Moody, who later wrote *Coming of Age in Mississippi*, staged a sit-in at the downtown Jackson Woolworth store. A gang of rage-filled white teenagers taunted them for three hours, squirting mustard and ketchup on their heads and finally beating, kicking, and spitting on them. They never fought back, instead relying on the media to report the incident nationally and ultimately bringing further embarrassment to a state widely perceived as backward.

On the other side were the militants. They couldn't just sit there passively while someone attacked them. They wanted to and did fight back the only way they knew how: with their hands. Constance Slaughter was one of those so-called crazy ones. I knew her quite well and had offered to help after she admitted that she couldn't read music in front of Pops. But she turned me down, seemingly content with pursuing her dream to become a doctor. Those were probably her last carefree days on campus. She met Medgar Evers on her first day and was willing to follow him anywhere. But he was murdered six days later, and she was devastated. From then on, she was about change by any means. She admits to having at least five or six fights with white male students while at Tougaloo.

Her greatest fight occurred during an Ol' Miss football game against the University of Houston. The night before, the black Houston football players stayed in the segregated Holiday Inn hotel. Constance and a friend went to meet the players. The next day, with the exception of the players and the peanut and beer vendors, the two women were seemingly the only two blacks in the sea of of about sixty thousand whites. It was her first game at Ol' Miss, a school she'd hated ever since the riot that had erupted over Meredith's enrollment. For her it turned out to be a pretty good game. One of her newfound friends broke away from the line of scrimmage and starting running down the field. Constance stood up and began cheering wildly, thoroughly enjoying the moment. As she turned her head down to say something to her friend, a beer bottle whizzed passed her face. The next thing she knew, a group of people were pulling her away from a sure beating. She climbed over people in a futile attempt to whip the boy who threw the bottle. She was swinging and crying at the same time, largely because she couldn't get her hands on the guy.

There were a lot of angry people walking around Tougaloo. When Medgar Evers was shot in the back near his front doorway on June 11, 1963, many students couldn't even attend his funeral. He was thirty-seven years old and we were younger, wanting to change not only segregation but the way in which white folks looked at and thought about us. Some wanted to burn everything in sight. The day before Evers's death, Alabama Governor George Wallace barred the admission of two black students into the University of Alabama. "I draw the line in the dust and toss the gauntlet before the feet of tyranny," Governor Wallace declared during his inaugural speech. "And I say segregation now, segregation tomorrow, and segregation forever." The Alabama crisis prompted President Kennedy to have an unplanned speech on civil rights shortly before Evers was shot down. "We are confronted primarily with a moral issue," President Kennedy said. "It is as old as the Scriptures and as clear as the American Constitution."

We were saddled with an incredible burden. Many of us were unable to enjoy our youth, unable to be free and uninhibited. We were mad and scared, determined to overcome yet unable to control our fragile circumstances. People drove by the campus on County Road at night, waving Confederate flags and firing their shotguns. No one was ever shot. Many of us thought it was a just a matter of time before a bullet had a Tougaloo student's name on it. We couldn't keep the trouble away from the campus forever. On one warm night in 1966, the school crowned Miss Tougaloo. It was one of the biggest events of the year, and the majority of the campus attended, wearing suits and polished shoes, pretty dresses and high heels. Somehow, a group of men drove past the front gate and planted a wooden cross in front of the president's house. They lit it on fire and sped away. The coronation had ended and many of us were leaving the gymnasium and headed toward our dormitory rooms when we discovered the cross burning inside the gates. Everything started happening at once. Someone spotted the pickup truck, and a few started running after it. Before long, everyone was running full speed, about two hundred of us, screaming and hollering, chasing the white men off campus. We felt so violated, so angry. We never caught them. I am not sure what we would have done if we had, but running after them provided a release for our conflicting emotions. We were hurt and disgraced, the burning cross reminding us of our powerless past and uncertain future. The cross symbolized our day-to-day reality: a constant battle against those on the wrong side of history.

There were too many tragedies. I remember awakening from a nap before choir rehearsal and walking downstairs. President Kennedy had been murdered and everyone was in a trance. "Now what are we going to do as a people?" I wondered aloud to someone. For the next few weeks, Pops worked us nearly to death. He had changed plans for the annual Christmas concert from Handel's *Messiah* to Mozart's *Requiem.* The runs in the Kyrie and later the Christe eleison had to be just right, and the lovely Lacrymosa had to have just the right lilt. The Rex Tremendae had to be majestic. He drilled and drilled us. It had to be right. The president had died. Seven months later, on June 21, 1964, James Chaney, Michael Schwerner, and Andrew Goodman were reported missing in Neshoba County, Mississippi. They were investigating the burning of Mount Zion Methodist Church, which the three civil rights workers had hoped to use for a summer freedom school, where they could give young rural blacks a basic education. Klansmen and Neshoba County Deputy Sheriff Cecil Price murdered and buried them in an earthen farm dam that had been under construction.

Politics had never mattered to me. Given the situation in Mississippi, I didn't quite see casting our lot with politicians. The ones I knew and read about were mostly liars and racists bent on keeping us undereducated and field workers. They resisted change and made voting all but impossible for those who sought change. For the most part, I remained politically neutral on campus, friends with everyone but loyal to my studies and music. I was not a radical. I didn't believe in protest just for the sake of protest. On one occasion, Birgit Nilsson, a well-known Swedish soprano, was scheduled to give a performance at the country fairgrounds outside of Jackson. I remember debating into the early morning hours how best to boycott the show because blacks were not allowed to attend. The tense racial climate caused Nilsson to cancel and we never executed our plans, but we were ready. Because of my nonalignment with any one group or cause, I was elected president of the student body during my senior year. Constance Slaughter was vice president. I conducted meetings in a very businesslike manner, much like the year before, when I was president of the Student Judiciary Committee. As such I was responsible for leading deliberations about student disciplinary hearings. On some occasions, we voted to expel students for major infractions, such as stealing or cheating. We also expelled the student who started a food fight in the cafeteria that quickly escalated into a full-scale riot. Some of them would come before the committee and try to persuade us with their black solidarity argument. I never bought it.

Even then, I never had time for foolishness. There was so much serious work to be done. Late in my junior year, I had scrapped plans of becoming a music teacher and began thinking about a career as an opera singer. It was the ultimate in singing. In the back of my mind, I was probably influenced by the fact that opera was considered highbrow, the music of the elite. My love for opera was more than simply status. Growing up as I did, I felt the importance of doing my best, striving for the ultimate. In a sense, all of us were trying to show the world that we were worthy. Nothing could deter us from striving to leave the cotton fields and escaping the perception that many whites and some blacks had about our capabilities. We wanted to be middle class. But as soon as we obtained one goal, we needed to reach another. It was as if the more progress we made, the wider the gap became. At one time, a high school education was a milestone. Then it was a college degree. For my particular field, I knew I needed graduate school. Manhattan School of Music accepted me, thus beginning a new challenge as an old one ended.

Sister Moten drove Mama up to see me graduate. Folding chairs were spread across the freshly cut lawn in front of Beard Hall, one of the oldest buildings on campus. It was a sunny day, and even the dignified guests used their programs to fan themselves as Tougaloo's ninety-seventh commencement began on May 29, 1966. My dark blue gown was laced with a gold rope that signaled that I had graduated cum laude. I felt that I now knew and understood the value of hard work. My efforts during the last four years had afforded me a college degree and a sense of accomplishment. No one could take that from me. Those of us in the choir rose up from our seats on the grass and walked over to the stage where Pops, decked out his cap and gown, led us through the Rex Tremendae movement of Mozart's *Requiem.* It was all very grand, unlike ceremonies today, where people shout and holler when their loved ones receive diplomas.

As far as we were concerned, the battle was not over, and that seemed to be the message of Dr. George Earle

Owen, the executive director of the United Christian Missionary Society in his commencement address, "How Big Is Your World?" If we had any doubt about what we could do as individuals outside of Tougaloo and, for that matter, Mississippi, Dr. Owen removed those self-imposed mental blocks and challenged us to not just pass through life but to grab all the success that we could. We were fired up when we left, humming the chorus to the school song:

> Tougaloo, Eagle Queen, we love thee
> Mother, Eagle, stir thy nest
> Rout thine eaglets to the breezes
> They enjoy the test.

A Budding Musician

THE SUMMER AND fall of 1966 were a glorious time to sing. I spent the summer after graduation in Chautauqua, a grand old city in western New York state filled with wide green lawns and tree-lined streets, wooden porches and rocking chairs. Some of the lovely homes had a view of Lake Chautauqua, many others had gazebos laced with ornate Victorian gingerbread. The natural beauty helped nourish a creative spirit in the city that had begun before the turn of the century, when Methodist Bishop John Heyl Vincent and Lewis Miller, a prominent industrialist and Thomas Edison's father-in-law, started a school for Sunday school teachers in 1874. Ulysses S. Grant vacationed there, and William Jennings Bryan gave inspirational talks attracting twenty-five thousand people. Years later, Chautauqua became known for its penchant for self-improvement, a spirit so bubbly that Theodore Roosevelt described it as "typical of America at its best."

I attended summer classes that were part of the Chautauqua Literary and Scientific Circle, a group that had begun by reading the great books of the Western tradition and later grew into an extensive summer calendar of lectures, concerts, and dramatic performances. For me, music was all day, every day: orchestral performances one night, operas the next. I spent most of my time learning repertoire at practice shacks in the music village. The library was bigger and better equipped with musical materials than the one at Tougaloo. I felt so blessed because I was fulfilling my dream of becoming a performing musician. The summer voice lessons were excellent. I learned the correct repertoire for my voice category and frequently sang in student recitals and tea parties for the rich and famous at the Atheneum Hotel. It was quite an experience, and for the first time in my entire life, I lived in a totally musical world.

Highbrow cultural events had not escaped the social mores back in Mississippi. They, too, remained segregated. The only person that I knew who ever tried to attend a music performance outside of campus was Bob Honeysucker, and he was arrested before he even had a chance to sit down. The Royal Philharmonic Orchestra from London, led by conductor Sir Malcolm Sargent, was scheduled to give the first concert of the 1963–64 series sponsored by the Jackson Community Concert Association. A group of Tougaloo students had appealed to the orchestra to insist that their concert be open to all or be canceled. The orchestra refused, prompting Dr. Elizabeth Sewell, a British citizen and a visiting professor at Tougaloo, to make a personal telephone call to Sir Malcolm. He claimed that racial problems in Mississippi were not his problem. To publicize the unfairness of Mississippi's high society, the student group, Cultural and Artistic Agitation Committee, decided to send an Englishman, Nicholas Bosanquet, who was visiting Jackson at the time to assist SNCC in voter registration, and Honeysucker. They presented their tickets at the door of the concert hall, and before they could take a step inside, police stopped them. The communication over the police walkie-talkies explained the situation: "Yeah, a colored man and a white one, but we got them and will take them right to jail." They never heard "The Star-Spangled Banner," the opening song; police had shoved them in the backseat, handcuffed, only to be released the next morning on bonds of $500 each. The British embassy later intervened and got the charges dropped. The incident made colorful reading in the *Manchester Guardian*.

Chautauqua indeed was a blessing and gave proof to the biblical passage "Ask and it shall be given unto you, seek and you shall find." I had realized by my junior year that Tougaloo was not offering all that I needed to become an opera singer. I certainly knew that I could attend a graduate school as a music educator because that was my major, and I was adequately prepared. But to sing, I needed something more. I went to the library at Tougaloo often and browsed through the music magazines. I came across a number of famous summer music institutes: Aspen, Interlochen, and Chautauqua. I talked with Dr. Borinski about my plans and decided to apply to all three. Bo-Bo, as most Tougaloo students called him, further told me that the chairman of the board of Tougaloo, Robert Wilder, had a summer home at Chautauqua and that I should strongly consider going to summer school there. As usual, money became an issue. I didn't have a dime and couldn't even afford the application fees, much less train fare to Chautauqua to audition for an opening. Somehow, Dr. Borinski came up with the fees for everything.

I attended my first summer session after my junior year. I met Robert Wilder and his wife, Ann, during the nine weeks of intensive music training. The Wilders had three small children at the time, and I was always at their cottage when I was not studying or working. I was offered a small scholarship, which paid for my lessons, but food, housing, books, and materials were my responsibility. I went to the Maintenance Department as soon as I arrived to ask about jobs. I was offered one cleaning toilets and public bathrooms. I grabbed the job. It was the only way I could survive my first summer. Someone found out that I was struggling and always broke. One night an old gentleman sat next to me in the amphitheater as the *Typewriter Concerto* was being performed. I had recognized the man, having seen him at a nearby church across from one of the outdoor toilets that I cleaned. He struck up a conversation. "You know, there is a person who asked me to give you this." He slipped $20 into my hand. I said thanks and asked if I could send the donor a note. The man quickly explained that the donor wanted to remain anonymous and that my success was all that he asked in return. During both of my summer sessions at Chautauqua, I received similar gifts and could only thank God for placing this unknown person in my life.

My teacher at Chautauqua was Josephine Antoine, a well-known soprano, who had a very fine career at the Metropolitan Opera. She was a very cordial woman, very fun-loving, and showered me with attention. I had told her that I was interested in attending graduate school, and she tried everything she could to support my plans. For one thing, she arranged an audition for me at the Eastman School of Music in Rochester, New York. By then, she had become a music teacher at the University of Arizona and had been invited to teach at the Eastman School. As is so often the case with male voices, she thought it better for me to learn under the tutelage of a man. One of her colleagues at Eastman knew the male tenor voice, and she wrote letters to him and other school officials about me and my potential during my senior year at Tougaloo. I remember catching the train from Chautauqua and riding seemingly forever to Rochester. Despite her efforts, Eastman and The Juilliard School rejected my applications. I had been accepted at Miami University in Ohio, and they offered a full scholarship, as did Washington University in St. Louis. But I wanted to attend a music conservatory. The Manhattan School of Music was the only one that afforded me an opportunity.

I had about a month before starting graduate school after my second summer session ended at Chautauqua. They awarded me a scholarship to pay for tuition, but that money did not cover living expenses. The least expensive place to live, the International House, was going to cost $700 a year. The Tougaloo connection came through again. I learned that Venora and Leroy Ellis, both graduates of Tougaloo and owners of a home cleaning business, lived in Westport, Connecticut, and had agreed to put me up until the beginning of school. Mrs. Ellis, a seamstress by trade, was a woman who could make ends meet. She and her husband truly cared about people—both of them were from Mississippi and had started their business from scratch. They were always eager to give Tougaloo students an opportunity during the summer to earn a little money before returning to school. I agreed to work for them in exchange for meals and a room in their basement. The Ellises had very wealthy clients who owned homes that were absolutely luxurious. I couldn't even dream of homes that opulent. Some of them had streams running through their backyards. Others had majestic Roman-style bathrooms. These people were truly living grand, and in every case, they were very, very kind. Most of them were Jewish, and despite their obvious wealth, it seemed to me that they had a special kind of bond with blacks as a result of their own struggle. There seemed to be an unstated understanding of what it meant to overcome. Invariably, three or four of us were sent to the house to work. The owners knew that many of us were college students and, to strike up a conversation, would ask about our future plans. After each house that I helped clean, I left a typewritten letter, introducing myself and describing my accomplishments and plans for the next school year. I further explained that I had a scholarship but did not have living expenses for the first year. If they saw fit, I asked, they could contribute. By the end of the month, I had raised more than $1,000 for my "living expenses fund," more than enough to pay for my room at the International House. Faith and hard work brought me through again.

My eyes were probably wider than most newcomers' when I arrived in the Big Apple. I saw the Empire State Building, and I remember always looking up for the first several days. I was totally oblivious of the dangers of big city life and was totally focused on school. I was truly a naïve country boy, but I never suffered because of my innocence. I remember the day that a man standing on 125th Street and Lenox Avenue tried to pull an old scam on me. He flashed a wad of money and asked if I could help him do something or other. An inner voice told me not to help this man out and I didn't, thank God. No telling what might have happened. In hindsight, it's amazing that nothing terribly evil did happen. Everybody must have known that I was green. I grew up in a trusting, nurturing atmosphere, where everyone was concerned about advancement. I didn't see the evilness of people, and instead chose to ignore most around me, unless they were concerned with music. I had so much work to do. Mississippi was considered to be one of the worst states in the country for education, and those statistics came from the predominantly white schools. Back then, only a few studies measured the education for blacks, and the results here was significantly lower. I felt a tremendous pressure to learn as much as I could; I always felt that I was behind and didn't know enough.

The Manhattan School of Music was small and a joy to attend. I knew on the first day that I had made the right choice. I was studying voice and taking lessons almost every day, attending classes in sight singing, music theory, and dictation. I was weak in music dictation, largely because the emphasis of a music major at Tougaloo was on music education rather than those skills. The aim was to prepare students to acquire jobs as teachers. To that end, the course offerings emphasized music history and research. I remember going over to Sam Goody on Fiftieth Street between Seventh and Eighth Avenues and buying my first record player in order to listen to the hundreds of pieces that I was required to know. The first recording that I owned was Mahler's Symphony no. 2, the *Resurrection* Symphony. Thanks to Miss Jones and Pops, I knew an enormous amount of choral music, which placed me far ahead of my classmates in that particular area. I attended conducting classes and knew practically all the scores, everything from Mozart's *Requiem* to Beethoven's *Missa Solemnis.* But there was never enough time in the practice rooms to learn all the new music in a tenor's repertoire. I auditioned for the school's opera theater and was selected to perform small roles at first. I was willing to do anything to gain as much experience as time allowed. I also found a new idol—Leonard Bernstein, the enfant terrible. I remember saving money to buy tickets to see him at Philharmonic Hall. I loved the way he conducted. He was so expressive, jumping up on the stage and coming down on the beat. I particularly enjoyed his interpretation of Mahler's Symphony no. 2.

My life was not entirely about work. One of the great things about attending the Manhattan School was that trustees frequently left free passes to the Metropolitan Opera. Those tickets were usually in the hands of Josephine Whitford, the dean of students. She was a little old lady with gray hair who seemed to take a special interest in me. She was one of the sweetest, gentlest women I have ever known. "Darling, how are you doing today?" she always asked. "Do you need anything?" She was just wonderful and made the difference between being lonely in New York City and having someone who cared. She continued the nurturing that I had received at Tougaloo and Coleman High. She often gave me tickets to the opera. Other times, she gave me score tickets, which enabled students to sit in the rafters. We could hardly see the stage but learned by following the score. Rarely did I get the chance to sit in the main hall; I considered a standing-room-only ticket as high cotton.

As for all young opera singers, it was important to be familiar with various roles—not just with the arias but the language and staging as well. That meant hours and hours of coaching and taking diction classes in French, German, Italian, Russian, and English. My first operatic apprenticeships occurred during the following two summers, when I was a member of the Lake George Opera Company preparing the role of Tamino in Mozart's *Die Zauberflöte* and the role of Alfredo in Verdi's *La Traviata*. Apprentices usually sang in the chorus and served as understudy to the lead roles. But every now and then some of us got a break, usually when the lead singer got sick. Colds and sore throats were normal, and when the Tamino lead at Lake George came down with the flu, I was asked to step in. The only problem was that I had already driven seven hours to New York City for the weekend and had to turn around and drive back. I did more than drive; I flew, gunning my little Dodge Colt to speeds of ninety miles per hour. Despite one speeding ticket, I made it back. This was my chance. Though I was never given the chance to stand in during rehearsal, I had been paying attention on the sidelines. I had studied the role completely. I had memorized the dialogue, the music, the staging, everything. Everyone thought that I had only twelve hours to prepare, but I already knew every move the tenor was supposed to make. I was the talk of Lake George and my colleagues after the performance.

The apprentice track was one way to gain operatic experience. The aim was to be heard by the right managers so that they could put you on their rosters, which would lead to work. Other options were traveling to Europe, if one had the money, and hoping that an opera house would offer a role. But one needed experience. Another way depended on having the good fortune of somehow gaining a well-connected mentor who could lobby and pressure well-placed officials in American and European houses to land roles. The reality of finding work was applying old-fashioned shoe leather: walking the streets and reading the newspapers and music magazines *Variety* and *Showbiz* for auditions. At that time, most of the area colleges had opera theaters, and I was able to perform for several of them, including the ones at Hunter College and Brooklyn College. At Hunter, I did Tamino again and at Brooklyn, I did a number of operatic roles, including Ferrado in *Così Fan Tutti* and Scarmuccio in *Ariadne auf Naxos.* I was also busy with the opera theater at Manhattan School of Music, where I did the role of Leandro in the opera *La Guerre* and covered the lead role in Busoni's *Arlecchino.* I sang lots of oratorios around New York City, including Haydn's *The Creation,* Mendelssohn's *Elijah,* Berlioz's *L'Enfance du Christ,* and a host of Bach cantatas.

New York City pulsed with creative energy. I lived in the International House, a ten-story building constructed in 1924 with money donated by John D. Rockefeller, Jr., and members of the Cleveland Dodge family. The house was founded to provide inexpensive rooms for about six hundred students from around the world. Half of the students were from America, and it was like living in a city within Manhattan. For a dormitory, it had everything: a thirty-six-piece in-house orchestra, lectures, movies, parties, free theater tickets, out-of-state trips, elegant public rooms, a pub, a gym, and reading and music rooms. The residential rooms were hardly luxurious, and the paper-thin walls encouraged students to participate in the activities. The building, on 122nd Street and Riverside Drive near Grant's Tomb, was near The Juilliard School, Riverside Church, and Columbia University and overlooked the Hudson River. Lots of famous people had lived there when they were students, such as Leontyne Price. Its location had an added advantage for me: Harlem was just a few blocks away.

Among the things offered in Harlem, churches were in abundance. Religion was still an important part of my life, and I wanted to make sure that I had a church home in New York. One day, while walking down the hill on 122nd Street, I noticed a church named Ephesus on 123rd Street and Lenox Avenue, in the center of Harlem. The name was special because it was the name of the church that my family belonged to in Greenville. Ephesus is also a significant name in biblical history. The apostle Paul wrote the epistles to seven churches, one of which was Ephesus. Ephesians, as we were called, were very proud of the significance of that name. The very strong attachment that I had to the church stayed with me through college and now graduate school. I remembered growing up and listening to the fire-and-brimstone sermons about the importance of keeping church in your life. Preachers urged us to remain a part of the Adventist church because if we didn't, we would surely be lost. That fear colored my entire life. The members of Ephesus Church in Harlem were warm and familiar, and for the most part, acted like the congregations of every other black church that I had attended over the years. They were fundamentalist to the bone and, now that I think about it, bourgeois to the bone, too. Shirt and tie were required, and any demonstrative praise was almost frowned upon. It was not unlike other so-called middle-class churches in Harlem where the black folk thought that it was low-class to praise God in any way that seemed African in spirit. Playing drums, shouting, and the throwing of hands were not encouraged. Dignity was defined by the times, and many back then appeared to want to run away from their blackness. There were those who were into black power and moving back to Africa, but some middle-class black folks didn't even want to hear gospel music on Sunday morning.

The church elders often asked me to sing. I always

thought that it was harder to sing for my people, though. They seemed to be more critical or at least less forthcoming with any kind of praise. Musicians in the church were rarely paid: they were willing workers but often not well trained. In most cases, a legacy of subpar music was the rule rather than the exception. The organ was never kept in good shape, and though it was a million-dollar-plus instrument, it was rarely tuned. Music always seemed to be an afterthought. It was a free-for-all, where instead of joyful noises, jealousies and petty politics rang loud. Nevertheless, Ephesus became my new church home after I transferred my membership from Greenville. I spent a lot of time with the youth programs and after a while, was asked to become the music coordinator for the youth church. I agreed, not really knowing what I was getting into. I was responsible for making sure that there was an organist, a pianist, and a choir or soloist every Sabbath for service. After a year, I gave it up. It was impossible to spend the necessary time to do a credible job, given my chaotic schedule with performances and graduate school.

One of the first secrets that I learned at Manhattan School of Music was to find a job as a paid singer at a church. I found one at the Trinity Episcopal Church in Southport, Connecticut. I had to wake up early Sunday morning and catch a train to Southport in order to sing as a tenor soloist. The pay was enough to make the trip and effort worthwhile. I sang for several other churches over the years, but Trinity was very special. The church had a boys choir, and I was very moved by their sound. Hearing them sing made me think about other boys choirs that I had listened to over the years. I was fascinated by the Berkshire Boys Choir, which was in residence at the Berkshire School near Tanglewood and often performed during the summer music season with the Boston Symphony. The choir selected the best boys from Anglican churches around the country and brought them together for a summer of recreation, music, and tutelage with one of the important English choirmasters.

My first talks about starting a boys choir at Ephesus Church began over dinner with the Thompsons in Brooklyn. They were members of the church and had two children, Lonieta and Marcus, both of whom were my age. Marcus had been the music coordinator at one time at the church. He was a first-rate violist and a student at Juilliard at the time. Unlike a lot of other musicians at the church, Lonieta was a real pianist and organist. She also studied at the Juilliard. We gravitated to each other because of our classical training. They frequently invited me over for Sabbath dinners on Saturdays, and we talked about people in the church and music. They were like family. One Sabbath, we were discussing the fact that my Sunday church gig was in Southport, Connecticut, and that they had a boys choir. The boys went to school at the Trinity Parish Church, very much in the style of the Western European tradition. The Ellises had introduced me to the director, Fred Dehaven, who answered a lot of my questions. I then began asking Ephesus Church officials about having one there. I was told that there had been one but it was only active for a couple of years. A young man named Bobby Bowman had organized the group, but he was later drafted into the army. His mother, Sister Bowman, had adopted me as a son, and I had talked with her about the choir. She also invited me over to her home in the projects on 116th Street and Lenox Avenue for Sabbath dinner. I would go over there, take a nap after dinner, and return to church in time for youth church. Marcus, Lonieta, and I decided that we should resurrect the boys choir and ask permission from Elder Carter, the minister at Ephesus. At the end of one Sabbath service, Marcus and I talked with Elder Carter. He promptly gave us his blessing without much discussion.

I advertised the first rehearsal in the church bulletin, and twenty boys came to the basement of Ephesus Church one Saturday afternoon. Ruth Nixon, a church member who had played piano for the former boys choir, agreed to accompany the new choir. She also brought her two sons. All the boys were sons of church members, and for the most part, well behaved, eager to sing. Some of the first boys were Mervin Lewis, Maurice Harvin, Leroy Williams, Alton Stewart, the Odom brothers, and the Boone brothers. Sister Callwood sent two of her older boys—she had four in all—to the first rehearsal. Her husband had died when the children were young, and she was trying to raise her sons in the church. They were of West Indian ancestry, and she was very caring, always calling me on the telephone, any time of day or night, to check on me. They lived in the Bronx, and their attitudes were always positive. They were poor but had dignity. The oldest brother, Sylvester, had a beautiful soprano voice. The next oldest, Delvin, could sing pretty well, but like most of the other boys that first day, his raw talent needed work. I asked them to sing a few songs and came away from the rehearsal with the feeling that I at least had something. The rehearsal wasn't memorable musically, but I was satisfied that they could sing, and more important, that they wanted to do something other than hang out on the streets.

Our rehearsals were held on Saturday afternoon at 4:00 P.M. Selecting the type of music was a problem. I had a vast knowledge of choral music for mixed choir based on my experiences as a chorister in high school and in college.

But I was not so well versed in music for treble voices. At first I chose mostly hymns. Of course the choir had little money of its own; most of the early expenses were paid from my meager pockets. Much of the music that we performed came from the catalog of the Galaxy Music Company, where I was working as a stock clerk. As the choir became better trained and I learned more music, we began performing music for mixed voices: soprano, alto, tenor, and bass. The repertoire included: The *Coronation* Mass in C of Mozart, *Amahl and the Night Visitors* of Menotti, the chorales of J. S. Bach, hymns, and a few original pieces composed by my friend Linda Twine. Linda and I met while pursuing our master's degrees at the Manhattan School. We were both performers, but just in case, we also were taking education courses in order to qualify as teachers in the New York City public school system.

The choir enthused the church. A core of sponsors donated $30 apiece and, in return, were listed in our programs. They also received tickets to choir concerts. Church policy precluded the sale of tickets, but we were able to pass out envelopes for volunteer offerings. We initially sang during services at Ephesus, and word began spreading in Harlem about the choir. Other churches began asking for our services. To meet the growing demand, I scheduled more rehearsals: one on Friday night and another on Sunday afternoon. I don't know where I found the energy. All of my time was spent between work on my master's degree, my part-time job at the Galaxy Music Company, my Sunday church job in Connecticut, and the choir. I was extremely busy and remember being exhausted all of the time.

My constant weekend schedule strained my relationship with my girlfriend, Betty. We had met at the International

House. An extraordinarily gifted soprano, she was a student at the Juilliard school in the opera theater. Even now, I can hear her constant refrain: "Walter and those boys." I spent a lot of time on the telephone, making sure that everyone showed up for rehearsals, and a lot of time in the library, researching music and boys choirs throughout the world. I demanded excellence in myself, and I wanted the same thing from the boys. They responded with few complaints. It was fun, and the kids had something to look forward to during the week. They were gaining a little fame and the younger kids in the church couldn't wait until they became of age to sing in the Ephesus Boys Choir. Some of my most memorable times were preparing for performances. Many of the deacons and elders who were fathers could sing bass and tenor and were the backbone of the choir. We performed Christmas concerts with orchestras and presented a whole host of material that at the time, quite frankly, we were not able to perform at the highest level.

Probably the most frustrating thing was my own lack of knowledge. There just wasn't enough time to do all of the things I wanted at the choir. By now, I had finished my master's degree at the Manhattan School of Music and had begun teaching at J.H.S. 99 in East Harlem. I worked full time as a music instructor and, because I was not a union member, crossed the picket line during the nine-week strike that began in September 1968. The strike paralyzed the city and divided the races. Particularly worrisome was the split between blacks and Jews, allies during the civil rights struggle of the late fifties and early sixties, but now increasingly at odds over sharing control of the schools and jobs. The original idea, decentralizing the nation's largest school system (1.1 million students, 900 schools, and a

55,000-member teachers union), was a good one. The idea was to give parents and community groups more control of the system. In New York, for example, 52 percent of the students were either black or Hispanic, while 90 percent of the teachers were white. The perception back then was that the majority of teachers came to the communities, made their money, and left. The teachers, it was thought, had little invested in the students' lives and, as a result, cared less about real academic progress. The theory and supporting arguments became extremely popular within liberal circles across the country and provided the Ford Foundation with enough evidence to award $135,000 grants to three predominantly black groups in New York City. The goal was to organize local planning boards to run public schools in their districts.

The state board of education approved the three experimental districts and gave the local boards responsibility for planning the curricula and recommending staff and budget matters. Theory met reality in the Ocean Hill–Brownsville section of Brooklyn. The local board ordered ten teachers to be transferred out of the district for a variety of reasons, including incompetence and opposing community control. That bold move infuriated about one hundred teachers, prompting them to walk out for several days to protest the lack of due process. The local refused to budge, and as the school opening approached in September, they decided not to allow the disgruntled teachers back into the classrooms. The strike was on, and for one of the first times in history, victimized whites took to the streets to protest the actions of blacks in power. The teachers union, led by President Albert Shanker, claimed the rights of teachers had been violated. Mayor John V. Lindsay was drawn into the battle.

He asked the Ocean Hill board to take the teachers back, which surprisingly they did, and the strike was called off.

At that point, when the teachers returned to their classrooms in Ocean Hill, the battle became hostile and vicious, polarizing the races and emotions of the city. The teachers said they were cursed, harassed, and in one case, threatened with death. The union immediately called another strike, this time adding another demand—that all who participated in acts of intimidation be removed from the schools. The predominantly Jewish teachers union saw the Ocean Hill district as a hothouse of militant, anti-Semitic, racist teaching. Shanker said he would not negotiate any agreement with the Ocean Hill board "because it would be like signing a nonaggression part with Hitler."

The lines broke down racially. The Ocean Hill board had the firm backing of blacks and Puerto Ricans, including the Congress of Racial Equality and the Black Panthers; the teacher's union had solid support from the white middle class. In November, more than two thousand people from white neighborhoods demonstrated at Governor Nelson Rockefeller's office, demanding the ouster of Mayor Lindsay, who they blamed for destroying the Ocean Hill school district. As a struggling musician, I had little choice. I couldn't afford to strike, and teaching was one of the few steady jobs I could find. I participated in various opera theaters after school, but that work was inconsistent. Many of the schools remained open throughout the strike, and we did what we could to provide the students with normal classes. I taught music appreciation. About one hundred junior high school students would come into the auditorium and hear a lecture and learn how to sing. Having a class of that size was counterproductive, but we kept them busy and involved.

I really didn't have any trouble from the picketing union members. A few of the teachers were called scabs, but it really didn't bother me. More troubling was my perception of the gap between the community's and the union's needs and their public positions. I felt that many of the community leaders were demanding power without knowing what to do with it. Many of them wanted control but had no idea how to control a school system, much less provide a secondary education. The union believed that community leaders were not responsible enough to run the system and would use personal biases to oust unwanted teachers. The truth was somewhere in the middle. The whole situation proved to be a disaster for learning. The strike was eventually settled after both sides agreèd to have a state board oversee the local planning board. The damage was lasting and probably created the first real wedge between blacks and Jews in New York City. It was one thing to march together in Selma; it was an entirely different matter to share power. I could see the effect in the children. Instead of learning, they became cynical, unmotivated. Who could blame them? That is what they saw in the adults.

I saw this attitude whenever I held auditions at public schools to find sopranos for the choir. The pool of singers at Ephesus had become shallower and shallower. Adding new blood to the choir created a problem within the church. Some of the members became agitated at the presence of nonmembers. Other problems began to surface, further straining my relationship with Ephesus. They complained about songs, characterizing a few pieces that I had selected as "worldly music." My choice of robes for the boys triggered the first outward sign of tension. A few of the parents considered the traditional cassock and surplice as too Catholic and thought they were the "mark of the beast." They quickly took their children out of the choir. They were so hypocritical; their sons would have dropped out anyway. Many would later hang out at the notorious bars on 125th Street.

The final blow came on January 9, 1969, when a fire ripped through Ephesus Church and completely gutted the interior, including the two-thousand-seat sanctuary. Fortunately, no one was injured, but the fire left church members without a place for worship. The parsonage, a building next door, was the only place where they could hold any of their activities, and the choir had to compete for time. The space was in great demand, and many of the older members constantly complained about the time given to the choir. While many people at Ephesus were very supportive, there were those who were downright hostile. Rehearsal time was becoming more and more difficult to schedule, and I needed to find another place.

The choir struggled there for a few more years until I finally decided that in order for us to have the necessary money for music and performances, the choir would have to incorporate as a nonprofit organization. At the suggestion of Debi Kops and Johann Elbers (who had given their services as program designer and photographer, respectively), I went to Volunteer Lawyers for the Arts, a nonprofit agency, and worked with Mr. Goldstein, a wonderful man who helped me navigate laws involving incorporating and establishing a board of directors. I also went to the Community Service Society, where I met Steve Simms. He was born and raised in Nebraska and was finishing his second year of graduate school at the Columbia University School of Social Work. He was assigned my case after I filled out a variety of forms at the office. He started putting together a strategy to identify and recruit potential board members. He also helped analyze the needs of the choir. At that time, our needs were simple—everything. We didn't have a board, nor did we have an organized process to find members. We needed to have people with a variety of professional skills, but more important, we needed people with good reputations within the art and corporate worlds who had access to money.

Steve was great and became like a brother to me. In addition, he was probably the only person whose feet were as big as mine. He told me where to find the names of foundations that might be willing to provide grants. He believed that if we could get people to come and see the choir perform and listen to their music, they would be hooked. These were not simply children singing songs; it was about saving lives, having a choir for the community to provide an alternative to what little many of them had. Steve understood my vision, and after he finished his work with the Community Service Society, volunteered to serve as head of the fund development committee. The choir was incorporated in November 1974, and the first board of directors was formed in February 1975.

I was not ready for the furor that followed at the church. When I mentioned the idea to Ruth Nixon and my desire to call the organization the Boys Choir of Harlem, she blew up. I will never forget her words. She was playing the piano when I told her about the newly created Boys Choir of Harlem, Inc. She stopped abruptly, turned to me, and said, "I don't want to have anything to do with the name Harlem in it." I was shocked. My mouth was wide open. I thought incorporating Harlem, with its grand tradition of music and the arts into the name was an honor. She quit, as did several other supporters. Many parents didn't want their children to be associated with those "worldly" boys that I had let into the choir. The Callwood brothers were two of the young men who stayed in the Boys Choir of Harlem. Sister Callwood and her two sons were leaders, and in fact, she allowed her two other boys to become choir members. They did what they thought was right, as did the parents who took their children out.

The politics were intense. There were differences within the same family. The most vivid occurred in a family where the father's support was unwavering, and he eventually became one of the first board members. His brother, on the other hand, wanted to exclude outsiders from the choir. Ephesus Church had many wonderful people who supported the BCH and its activities. Paramount among them were the parents of the boys themselves. Sister Sally Boone, the first Parents Association president, had two sons who remained in the choir—Kenneth and Michael. Michael was a wonderful pianist who eventually went to the Eastman School of Music. Some years later, when the BCH was instituting a program for gifted students, I hired Michael to be project director. Michael was a wonderful person, but office work was not his forte. He had majored in the bass viola at Eastman and eventually played bass for Ben Vereen's band. Michael married and moved to Philadelphia. Kenneth was the outgoing one. Last I heard, Kenny was working for a New York City bank and producing his own recordings. There was also Sister Anderson, who had two sons in the choir, Robert and Anthony. Robert had one of the most gorgeous voices and was smart but always more eager to be a part of the crowd. Anthony was shy and grew to be over six feet tall and a collegiate basketball star. They had a sister, Sheila, who went to law school. Robert went to the navy.

Word of mouth eventually led me to Mr. Hansborough,

director of the Marcus Garvey Community Center, a relatively new recreation center on Harlem's Mount Morris Park. The park was once considered one of the jewels of New York. It has the highest peak in Harlem, and there was an iron bell tower at the top. The view from on high seemingly erased the urban blight and summoned one back to Harlem's glory days.

The village of Nieuw Haarlem, founded by the Dutch in 1658, grew by the eighteenth century into a wealthy suburb where Alexander Hamilton and other aristocrats built their homes. By the early twentieth century, with wide, tree-lined boulevards, its rolliing topography, many parks, and central location, Harlem became the choice place of residence for such rich New Yorkers as the Astors, the Baileys, (of Barnum and Bailey's Circus), and Houdini. Real estate speculators overbuilt Harlem in the 1900s, and faced with an economic bust and a steady exodus of whites to the suburbs, the speculators began to fill their elegant brownstones with blacks leaving the South. By 1920, Harlem was a predominantly black neighborhood, and in the giddy days of the postwar decade, it exploded with music, dance, poetry, and politics. Langston Hughes wrote verse to the "dusky sash across Manhattan." Marcus Garvey gathered thousands to his Back to Africa movement. Here were W. E. B. Dubois, Paul Robeson, Scott Joplin, Joe Louis, Dizzy Gillespie, Asa Philip Randolph. The Harlem Renaissance was alive and flowing, causing Duke Ellington to summon "Take the 'A' Train" to Harlem, which had become more of a spirit than simply an address. The spirit endured over the years, even after the once grand boulevards fell victim to urban blight. Harlem never lost its allure.

One of the first official pictures ever taken of the Boys Choir of Harlem was shot on that hill around the bell tower. Mr. Hansborough was very gracious and gave us our first rehearsal space outside of Ephesus Church. The Garvey Center was not without its problems. The center's piano was always out of tune and many of the keys didn't work. The piano rested on a dolly, making it difficult to find a chair that was tall enough for someone to sit and play. The building was always cold, and we often rehearsed bundled in our coats and scarves. Even though we didn't have much, our ambitions were high. We never canceled a rehearsal. We learned Britten's *Missa Brevis in D* and a host of new songs written or arranged by Linda Twine and Lee Cooper—songs that were more popular, such as "Mr. Bojangles," "Straighten Up and Fly Right," and "I Believe in Music." The kid I remember most from that group was Terrance Henderson. He was eventually swept up by the Hotchkiss School and ended up at the University of Pennsylvania.

It was at the Garvey Center that Franklin Williams, the longtime civil rights activist who had become the American ambassador to Ghana, came up one afternoon to hear the boys rehearse. His interest would vacillate for the next twenty years. The idea was to ask Williams to become chairman of our board. He was president of the Phelps Stokes Fund, a foundation dedicated to improving education for American Indians, blacks, and Africans. He was very well connected. A graduate of Lincoln University, Williams was an accomplished lawyer, working for a while with his fellow alumnus Thurgood Marshall and appearing before the U.S. Supreme Court, winning reversals for several young blacks facing the death penalty. He later helped establish the Peace Corps and became the first black to be named to the U.N. Economic and Social Council.

We met him in his office. I don't think he was impressed

initially, but he did promise to visit the choir at the Garvey Center and consider how he could help. The real power in getting Williams's attention was his executive assistant, Shelby Howatt, who became a longtime friend and staunch supporter of the choir. Williams swept into the Garvey Center in very grand style, listened to the kids, and promised to help. After his visit, we constantly talked with Shelby, who persuaded Williams to host a reception for a few important people to help us establish a board of directors. We held the reception on February 14, 1975, at the Phelps Stokes Fund. The boys performed next door at the Liederkreis Foundation Building.

The reception was significant because we were able to reach a number of people who, without Williams's clout, would have never given us the time of day. In attendance were Judge Oliver Sutton (who at board meetings would write out a personal check, throw it out on the table, and challenge others to do the same), the Honorable Percy Sutton (who was then Manhattan borough president), Jane Boyer, Kent McKamy, Robert Saintangelo, Ida Smith, and Steven Simms. Our plans, though, went awry: Williams refused to become chairman of the board. He believed that we were still green, and he couldn't afford to lend his name to our fledgling organization. He said he would help in any other way that he could. We were left to fend for ourselves with a new board and no leader. Williams was never directly involved, but we would keep him updated on our progress. We held our board meetings for a while at the Phelps Stokes Fund and used their facilities whenever else we needed to have a nice, safe location. We began to raise money, and from time to time, Williams would give the BCH a grant from his discretionary funds. The long road and constant struggle for the Boys Choir of Harlem had begun.

The Sound of Harlem

THE SOUND OF the Boys Choir of Harlem was the subject of debate from the very beginning. Our sound—that of black voices—was indeed different but no less legitimate than a European sound. Our diction was clean, our pitch was pure. I refused to allow anyone to persuade me to have a Viennese, German, or English sound. I was convinced that the young men in Harlem could remain true to the tradition of the boys choir without sounding European. I didn't come to these conclusions quickly or easily, and our sound remains an issue in some circles.

The European sound was an acquired taste for me. I knew and felt more comfortable with a darker one that stirred my soul through high school and college. I also knew the work required to bring out the best in my own voice. Admittedly, my exposure to other kinds of sounds was limited; segregation stole musical variety from my youth. Recordings were my only exposure to classical music. I saw and heard my first live performance at Touga-

My mother's mother, Mary Green.

The three women who raised me. (Left to right:) "Li'l Mamma," a family friend; Sammie Holland, "Aunt Nannie"; and my mother, Lena Green.

My first bicycle.

My younger brother, Horace, at age 10.

I played a groom during an elementary school play for the Seventh Day Adventist Church.

The gates at Tougaloo College.

*Ariel "Pops" Lovelace, conducting the Tougaloo College Choir during a perfor-
mance at the school chapel. I sang tenor in the front row.*

The first official photograph of the Boys Choir of Harlem, taken in 1975 at the Bell Tower on Mt. Morris Park overlooking Harlem.

A rehearsal at the Church of Intercession gymnasium.

Performing in 1975 for First Lady Rosalyn Carter at the Guggenheim Museum in New York City.

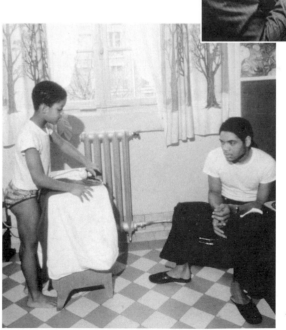

Two choristers prepare for performance at an orphanage where we stayed in Paris.

Our 1980 performance at the Notre Dame Cathedral in Paris.

The boys will always remember their Christmas concert at the St. Baavo Cathedral in Haarlem, Holland—they had to wear their coats underneath their gowns and, as a result, called the beautiful building "St. Cooldo."

We were all smiles before our performance at Notre Dame.

Several choristers purchased "African" walking sticks before our performance in Jamaica in 1984.

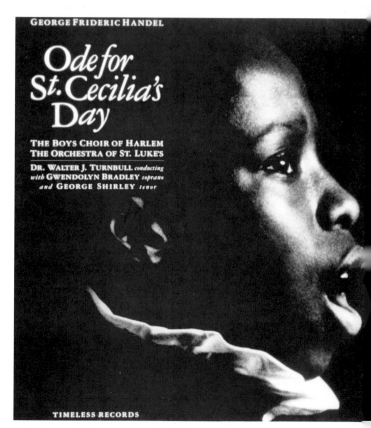

GEORGE FRIDERIC HANDEL

Ode for St. Cecilia's Day

THE BOYS CHOIR OF HARLEM
THE ORCHESTRA OF ST. LUKE'S
DR. WALTER J. TURNBULL *conducting*
with GWENDOLYN BRADLEY *soprano*
and GEORGE SHIRLEY *tenor*

TIMELESS RECORDS

The cover of the Boys Choir of Harlem's first classical recording.

loo when the St. Olaf Choir, directed by Heinz Christiansen in Minnesota, shared their unique and wonderful voices during a concert. I had never heard a sound like that before and had mixed feelings. It was a white sound, very straight, with little vibrato. It was totally opposite of the one that I had grown to love.

I tried to get my boys to have that classic European sound for years. It never sounded right. I wanted the natural sound I heard in Leontyne Price. I heard it on radio stations playing rhythm and blues, and I heard it over the telephone. There is something unique and warm about the black voice that has nothing to do with diction and is clearly distinguishable. Some may argue that differences in head structure and nasal passages may explain our sound. Either way, one of the most peculiar practices of attending conservatories is that teachers there often try to change what they consider unfamiliar. No one had developed a standard for black voices. Though a certain amount of flexibility is afforded the voices of soloists, choral music styles are largely measured by a Western European yardstick. I needed to expand those limits and define our sound within the context of the black experience, where hallelujah has a different ring, a soul of its own.

Gwendolyn Brooks captured the essence of classical music in Harlem in "The Sundays of Satin-Legs Smith":

> Down those sore avenues
> Comes no Saint-Saens, no piquant elusive Grieg,
> And not Tschaikovsky's wayward eloquence
> And not the shapely tender drift of Brahms.
> But could he love them? Since a man must bring
> To music what his mother spanked him for
> When he was two: bits of forgotten hate,

Devotion: whether or not his mattress hurts,
The little dream his father humored: the thing
His sister did for money: what he ate
For breakfast—and for dinner twenty years
Ago last autumn: all his skipped desserts.

The pasts of his ancestors lean against
Him. Crowd him. Fog out his identity.
Hundreds of hungers mingle with his own,
Hundreds of voices advise so dexterously
He quite considers his reactions his,
Judges he walks most powerfully alone,
That everything is—simply what it is . . .

We started small. We had about twenty boys and a budget of about $20,000 shortly after we incorporated, the money largely from individual donations. I earned $200 per week and supplemented my income by driving a cab. My part-time assistant, Aisha Farid, earned $125 per week. Our mission was not unlike those of the European boys choirs. They pursued excellence in music and acquired the habits of responsibility, attention to detail, personal discipline, and appreciation of the beautiful. As in Europe, the minds of the boys in Harlem had to be clear and focused on achieving excellence in music. But factors outside of the choir cluttered several young minds, affecting our ability to make music. I realized early on that I needed to address a variety of problems. I saw kids that were not doing well in school and realized that I needed tutors and counselors. Logistical problems also began mounting. We needed a warm, safe place to rehearse. The need to audition and find new boy choristers in the ghetto generated a constant stress. The search for funding was never-ending. Willie

Gonzales, one of Steve Simms's friends, introduced me to a writer, Roger Olsen, who wrote proposals for ASPIRA. Olsen and I spent hours writing grant proposals during weekends to the New York Council on the Arts, the Department of Education, and small foundations. The grants slowly trickled in, usually in amounts ranging from $500 to $1,000.

We still had shows to do. I remember how frantic we were, rehearsing like crazy before our first big performance at St. Paul's Chapel on April 5, 1975. The show went off smoothly, and for the several hundred people who attended that night at Columbia University, it was their introduction to the Boys Choir of Harlem. We had an orchestra and opened with Mozart's *Coronation* Mass in C. After intermission we showed the variety that has become our trademark by singing a Xhosa folk song, a Swahili lullaby, and "Mister Bojangles" along with several other popular songs arranged by Linda Twine and Lee Cooper, who wrote our signature piece, "We Are Heroes."

One of the people in the audience was the Reverend Frederick Boyd Williams, rector of the Church of the Intercession. He told me after the show that he had fallen in love with the choir and was willing to do anything he could to help us out. Father Williams was doing more than simply talking. Within a few months, the Boys Choir of Harlem had a new home—the Church of the Intercession, a beautiful English Gothic cathedral, built in 1907, complete with ninety-foot ceilings and soaring columns. The huge free-standing tower could be seen from miles away. We had an office and use of the choir room.

Our needs, as Jesse Jackson liked to say, were as varied as our skin tones. I listened more than I talked, letting the stories of the boys unfold. I nurtured the gifted, encouraged the average. I did all that I could, but in some cases, I was unable to prevent what their often dysfunctional environments seemed to dictate. It was one thing to purchase winter hats and scarves, as I did for all the choir members when we rehearsed at the chilly Marcus Garvey Center; it was an entirely different matter to reverse generations of urban pathologies. Though many were still able to persevere, others dropped out for a variety of reasons. Each provided a lesson for me, and I could only conclude that I needed to spend more time, provide more services, develop more programs. I thought that I could save every child that I taught. I was naïve.

They begin as angels, little brown faces with sweet little voices. Billy Green was a fourth grader when he started with the choir. He was considered the school menace, the child most likely not to succeed. I seldom trusted those sorts of judgments; I knew what teachers had said about me as a student. I was willing to give everyone an opportunity. I strongly believed then, as I do now, that development doesn't occur in a child on demand. It takes time and patience, and with encouragement and discipline, the seed of striving for excellence could be planted. Billy tested my beliefs. He came from a neighborhood that was not in the mainstream of drug trafficking. He had a very strong sense of family and community and came from a household where everyone worked. His natural mother left him when he was six months old. His upbringing fell into the hands of an aunt, several cousins, and a grandmother. He was well kept and well fed, but Billy had a real attraction to the mystery of the streets. He was a trendy kid, always wearing the latest fashions. He was physically and mentally tough, rarely refusing to back down from a fight, and, more often than not, welcoming trouble. When it was discovered that he had a talent, his stock went up, and everybody around him, including the same teachers who had labeled him a troublemaker, immediately encouraged him to become a part of the choir. I told him that rehearsals were usually after school, attendance was mandatory, and unruly behavior was simply not tolerated.

Of course, he required supervision and disciplining after he arrived at the choir. By then, I had already established a summer program, where I would take the children to a camp for intensive music training and fun. It was a way for them to get out of New York City and live in the country for several weeks. Billy had attended two of these camps and was beginning to understand the system at the choir. But Billy did not believe enough in himself to go all the way across and become a full-fledged performing member. His attitude was fine toward people he felt comfortable with, but if he thought you were looking down on him, he wouldn't speak to you. You had to earn his respect and approval; only then would he begin to show some of his vulnerabilities. Over time, after several talks, Billy had evolved to the point where he started to let down some of the defenses of the street and be more of an even-tempered person. By the time he reached that point, he had started attending P.S. 164, a rough junior high school, where he fell in with the wrong crowd. He played hooky from school, and his attendance at rehearsals was inconsistent. He would stop coming for a few days, only returning after I would go to his house and talk with his aunt to keep him involved.

But the lure of the streets became too much. Billy became a follower and life began to go downhill. He dropped out of the choir. He would visit on occasion to reaffirm his past connection. I always told him that he could come back, that there was an open door for him. He would try for a few days and then fizzle out. It wasn't as if Billy didn't have positive qualities. His strength was his ability to size people up, to figure out if they were real or phony. But his weakness was his lack of belief in himself. His determination to succeed at the choir gradually petered out, and he began selling crack. The money and the excitement just overwhelmed him, and every now and then, I would see him on the corner at night, dealing. I'm quite sure he was also using. One of the lures of dealing is that for every ten vials of crack sold, one is free. It was heartbreaking to even think about little Billy using crack. It got to the point where if I saw him, he would run away from me to avoid making eye contact.

Daniel Zellman was Jewish and one of the few whites that we had at the choir. He was in the fourth grade at P.S. 28 and was the type of child who was not afraid of new experiences. He was a smart boy, very trusting, and our relationship was not one between a black and a white but rather between a teacher and a student. The color of his skin was of no particular significance to me. His father and especially his mother were very excited about having him in the choir. They were from Israel and had grown up on a kibbutz. His mother was considered to be a black Jew and the father a white Jew. She felt close to people of color and trusted her child in our care. Daniel was very impressionable, and because his family assured him that everything would be all right, he felt comfortable in Harlem. Daniel was always very cheerful, upbeat, really spry all the time. He lived in a neighborhood that was predominantly Jewish in a section of Manhattan known as Washington Heights.

He caught the bus to Harlem by himself, leaving his relatively safe neighborhood to venture into a predominantly black world. Daniel would pass drug dealers and crowds of people and street action. The mother viewed this as her son's introduction into the real world; she felt that it was important for him to see that the world was a place where the majority of people were struggling, not one where life was always very calm and manageable. She wanted him to understand reality, whereas the father wanted to cushion him more.

Daniel was an only child and very creative. When he came to camp one summer, he won a major contest in which the children had to create a character and then silently act as the character. Daniel was surprised that he won. He was the only white person there and had automatically assumed that everyone would vote for another black person. But when he won, he suddenly realized that there was fairness, that he had won this contest in spite of the fact that he wasn't black. From that moment on, Daniel was sold on the Boys Choir of Harlem. He realized that he was surrounded by people who accepted him for who he was and understood and respected his creativity. He came back the following fall, eager to participate. But his mother and father openly disagreed about the amount of time he spent at the choir. They eventually took him out. They moved back to Israel to live on a kibbutz, despite the mother's objections. They were part of the first group of Jewish New Yorkers to settle on the Gaza Strip in the West Bank.

Randy Smith lived with his mother and grandmother in the St. Nicholas housing developments, one of the roughest, most violent, drug-infested projects in New York City. He came from P.S. 154, located one block away. Most of the children there were quickly labeled as incorrigible: they didn't want to learn, didn't want to work, and aspired only to become drug dealers and thieves. Unlike Daniel Zellman, Randy could not simply pass through the projects. He lived there and had to develop a tough urban veneer to mask his joy at being in the choir. He was in the fourth grade when he auditioned and a very fine treble. He also had a very pleasant temperament, always trying to do the right thing. Most of the ten-year-olds he was growing up with were busy sneaking on the A train behind the St. Nicholas projects and riding two stops to Forty-second Street, where they frolicked among the urban filth of pimps, prostitutes, drugs, and dirty book stores. The Deuce, as the seedy section of New York is called, became their playground, their backyard. Randy had a dilemma. He faithfully came to rehearsals, but he couldn't tell any of his neighborhood friends, most of whom respected only rappers and criminals. I remember walking home with Randy one day along 127th Street. As some of the neighborhood boys came along, Randy whispered: "Shh, shh, shh. . . . Don't tell them I'm in the choir." I played along with him but realized his conflict was real. We talked the next day about his lack of pride in the choir. He told me all of the sordid things that the other boys were doing. If he told them about singing in the choir, they would think he was attending church or, worse, that he was a sissy.

Randy had problems right from the start. For whatever reason, some of the kids called him "Bonehead." He wore very thick glasses and one day he broke them. Randy's mother stopped bringing him to rehearsals for a while as a result. After a few absences, I called her for an explanation, and she then told me about the broken glasses. She believed that he needed them in order to be successful. Without the glasses, she thought, Randy couldn't sing or see a blackboard. I tried to be as gentle as I could but I strongly urged her to bring Randy in the next day. I would replace the glasses. She brought him in, and he learned how to take the subway from St. Nicholas to make rehearsal. Most of Randy's reservations about the choir disappeared after he attended summer camp. He got the chance to do several things that he had rarely done before: eat three meals daily, have a clean room, and cool off in the water of a swimming pool rather than that from an illegally tapped fire hydrant. And probably for the first time in his life, he heard silence at night, instead of gunfire or people banging on doors, hollering, "Let me in, let me in." He realized that the choir could offer him something other than what his neighborhood provided.

Randy had more than his neighborhood to overcome. His family was filled with problems. Several of his relatives were dealing drugs, so much so that his grandmother refused to allow any of them in her apartment. We later discovered a problem with his mother. At the time, we gave parents envelopes to collect donations or money from ticket sales. Randy's mother would receive the money and keep it. The situation was bad. I had to ask her to stop soliciting in the name of the Boys Choir of Harlem, particularly when there wasn't even an event. She became very angry and suddenly pulled Randy from the choir. We never told Randy about his mother. His slide was almost immediate. By then, he was attending junior high school and had to be held back a year. He could not redirect any of his creative energy and discipline. No other positive extracurriculars existed for him. Still, he had his past experience with the choir, and he knew that he didn't have to be a hoodlum. After about two years of being away, he decided on his own to come back to the choir, despite his mother's objections. But he was surrounded by his dysfunctional family and bad luck. His mother was asked to leave the St. Nicholas projects and they were living in a homeless shelter in Brooklyn for a while. Randy's mother suffered a severe asthma attack shortly after that and died. Her death caused Randy to start becoming fatalistic about a lot of things, and when his grandmother became very ill, he thought that he would lose her, too. Randy kept working, though, regaining his position as a tenor in the performance choir. He had dedicated his efforts to the memory of his mother, and it paid off. He would later attend my alma mater, Tougaloo College, and because of his extraordinary talent, he received the benevolence of a wealthy patron of the Boys Choir of Harlem, much as I did when I attended Chautauqua.

Single-parent children had special problems. One of them was what I called "faceless fathers." These were men who fathered children and then disappeared, only to resurface and manage to influence their children from a distance, usually at critical periods in their children's lives. Paul Butler had such a father. When he started with the choir, he was an average-size kid for a fourth grader, very pleasant for the most part, not wanting to stick out or stand out. It seemed he just wanted to be an average person. He was living in a very rough section of Harlem, on Lenox Avenue and 143rd Street, with his mother, father, and younger sister. His mother worked as an attendant at Harlem Hospital; his father was a street vendor. He sold what he considered to be reputable merchandise. His wife did not see him as a consistent breadwinner and decided to leave him. The separation occurred when Paul was in the fifth grade, and he and his younger sister sided with the mother. At that point, the mother really depended on the BCH as a positive activity for her son. More important, she wanted to provide her son with male leadership and role models who had a strong sense of what men ought to do and be about.

Over the years, Paul would have better material things than many of the kids around him. His motivation to succeed, however, dwindled. He looked for easy answers. At that point his father suddenly became important to him. He saw him as an example of a man who was using his street knowledge to make it from day to day. That was the kind of information Paul wanted, and he believed that his father was the only one who could teach him those survival skills. Paul once looked for sure ways to get ahead; he later looked for the easy way out. By the time he entered high school, he was influenced by a strong drive to have money in his pocket all the time. That became the symbol of potency. Having money meant that he could be his own person, and what was happening at BCH was delaying his rite of passage to manhood. Paul had a very fine voice and worked pretty hard. He was very honest and would tell the truth even when he had made a mistake. But he remained reluctant to ask for help. He thought that he could solve all his problems and overcome his weaknesses all by himself. I remember him waiting for me outside my office so he could show me his report card. He had received good grades that semester and wanted to prove that he could fend for himself. He would later attend Central State University. His unwavering honesty confirmed what I already knew: single-parent children are capable of having values, too.

It remains a mystery to me, though, why some kids from

single-parent families have home training and others don't. Even within the same families, the values of children can be completely different, as in the story of Richard and Joseph Jones. They came to the boys choir as a result of their cousin, who was one of the first members in the choir after we left Ephesus Church. Richard and Joseph were raised by their mother, who had had older children by different men. Richard and Joseph were the product of the same father. Their mother was a real go-getter, always working several jobs and seldom at home. She had lost all three of her brothers to drugs and urban shoot-outs. One of the brothers was arrested in front of Wilson's Restaurant in Harlem. He had tried to bribe a police officer with $10,000. The officer later found a suitcase in his trunk filled with cash. The mother's oldest brother was serving time in prison and was later killed by another inmate with a home-made knife. The youngest brother was shot dead in the street in uptown Manhattan. While the brothers were living, they gave money to Richard and Joseph. Richard knew them, but Joseph was too young to remember them. Nonetheless, he always talked about the uncles he never knew.

As is often the case, Richard had to take care of Joseph, who needed more than a child's supervision. Joseph was very sweet, very kind, jovial, always smiling. Richard was always very serious and felt later in life that he never experienced the joy of childhood. His resembled mine, and I knew there was truth to his feelings. They lived in Brooklyn and had to travel about an hour by subway to make rehearsals. Richard would eventually graduate from high school, attend Fisk University for a number of years, and later join the military. He also would come back to the Boys Choir of Harlem and serve as an intern. He was one of the kindest young men that I have ever met.

Joseph, on the other hand, was a completely different story. He needed so much attention. I gave him as much as I could but my efforts were futile. He came and went as he pleased. While he was a talented kid, his biggest weakness was that he needed someone else's okay, someone else's blessing. He finally left the boys choir after he tried his hand at being the class clown: he pulled his penis out during a rehearsal. I didn't know about the incident until later. A few of the kids told me, and then we had to deal with his disruptive behavior. We placed him on a special, heavily supervised schedule, and he still couldn't get it right, eventually dropping out. His brushes with the law become more frequent and serious. Simple drug possession charges were first. Weapons charges came later. I remember him and his mother coming to us for support. We wrote letters on his behalf to his probation officer and several judges to no avail. He later ran away from his mother and moved in with his father, who he had never seen before. Before long, he was involved with the drugs near 150th Street, where his father lived.

Another set of brothers that we had were the Gateses, Alex and Terry. Terry was the older and his mother initially brought him to an audition. He was about eleven when he started. Alex, who everyone called "Junior," came to the audition with them at the Church of the Intercession. I asked about the little one, if he wanted to sing. He must have been eight years old at the time, much younger than we usually take them. Both brothers were extremely talented, especially Alex. But what impressed me the most about their mother was that she needed somebody to babysit. She was pushing me to take both of them. She was thirty-three, a single parent, and had a job as a secretary.

She had a daughter, too, but she was definitely trying to get these boys out of her hair. When they entered high school, she was pushing them to get out of the house and start working. She wanted to get on with her life, and there was a lot of conflict within that family over who was going to work and bring in money. Terry would eventually drop out of the High School of Music and Art, a specialized school in New York City. We helped him enroll in a GED program, which he completed. He then joined the army.

Terry was always the more responsible one. He was in charge of taking care of Alex, who from the beginning was very disoriented and sloppy. We used to get on Alex about how he ate at the table. He was just a pig. He would have cookies in his pocket and eat with all ten fingers. In later years Alex became so prim and proper at the table that it looked funny, because back then Alex might pick up a soup spoon and do anything with it. He was very talented and sang solos for the choir. He had a very nice gospel-type voice and could also use his head voice as in the Western European tradition. Once they were teenagers, both of them eventually dropped out because, as I've said, their mother wanted them to start earning money. We had found Alex work through the Job Corps. He also had dropped out of high school. We helped him acquire a GED. He was working odd jobs in the city for a while, then survived a gunshot wound to his head. He would later die from an undetermined disease.

Many of these children were vulnerable, sent out in the world without the necessary emotional strength to make correct choices. They needed more than the attention afforded by most New York public school teachers. There were times when I could provide it, other times when I couldn't. I didn't have enough money or people to bridge the gap between what some of the children needed and what I could offer. Chris George was one of those kids who fell between the cracks. He was not a particularly quick boy, and his singing suffered as a result. His mother was an incurable alcoholic. His father left her and took his three sons with him. He was forced to resign as a New York City police officer because of some unknown incident that rendered him unable find another "good" job afterward. He was, of course, suing the police department. We learned that he drove a cab, but he never really told us what he did for a living. Chris was basically raising himself. Only two years separated Chris from his older brother, who also was raising himself. The father did not have a routine or a structured environment; he was always grabbing at straws, driving his cab up to eighteen hours a day to make up lost income. They were more like brothers than father and sons. Chris told me several times that he couldn't depend on his family to help him navigate through life; the environment just wasn't there. His older brother was left in charge of the house and was supposed to monitor Chris's comings and goings. His mother lived in Brooklyn and became less and less of a figure in his life. His father told him at one point to forget about her. In the several meetings we had with Chris and his father, the man never once mentioned using the family as a support group to help his wife get better. He seemed to be willing to let her remain an alcoholic, and Chris was caught in the middle, not knowing what to do or say, torn between his love for the woman who gave him life and his need for the support of his father.

Chris's other brother, a year older than he, had been shot to death. The shooting occurred about two months before Chris joined the choir. He showed no signs of trauma or any feeling as a result of the shooting. It was almost as if he had resigned himself to believe that his brother was in the wrong place at the wrong time, that it was his fault, and that's the way it goes. Chris didn't know much about the details of the shooting. Nevertheless, he figured that his brother should have known better. That sort of reaction from Chris was typical; his emotional development was nowhere near his social and intellectual skills. He believed that he did not have to live the way his peers did because he was his own person. He, too, eventually dropped out. We could no longer depend on him to attend rehearsals, and then his father was kicked out of their apartment. He was unable to pay the rent. Chris went to live with his aunt in the Bronx; his brother moved in with their mother in Brooklyn. The last time I saw Chris, he was high on drugs, standing on a corner in the Bronx. He still comes to the choir every now and then. He wants to maintain a hold on the one thing that was stable in his life. He came into my office recently and said that he remembers some of the lessons that we tried to teach during rehearsal. "You told us that one day in the future, each of us would come back to the choir and tell you that you were right," he said. "Well, I'm here to tell you that you were right."

Not all of the children succumbed to the streets. Phillip Brown is a success story. He was raised by his grandmother and his great-grandmother. He had a very nice attitude, always positive, and frequently called me Dad. I don't remember very many times that I had to get after him as a kid. He was fourteen when we auditioned him at P.S. 195. Frankly, I was a little surprised when he showed up for his first rehearsal at the Church of the Intercession. He didn't show any enthusiasm at all. He was a little chubby at the time, and some of the kids called him Teddy Bear. Music was a struggle for him. Seemingly, he could never sing on pitch, a problem the boys turned into a new nickname, Pancake. He stuck with it, though, and earned his spot in the performance choir, going to Europe and later Japan.

Phillip lived in the southern part of Harlem, near 116th Street and Eighth Avenue, which was one of the major drug-selling areas. He lived one block from there and was a loner. No one from the choir lived there, and most of the kids his age were either dropping out of school or selling drugs. He had developed a strong sense of direction, virtually on his own. His mother and father had separated but both lived near their son. Phillip didn't visit his mother very often but knew where she lived and how to get there. His father had moved in with another woman. Within an eighteen-month period after his arrival at the choir, tragedy struck twice—both his father and his great-grandmother died. Phillip had to be strong. His grandmother, who had to bury both her son and her mother, leaned on him for strength. Phillip was forced to wear a smile even when he wanted to break down. His ability to persevere was one of his greatest assets. He was honest about himself, readily admitting that he was not fully developed emotionally. He knew he had to grow and confronted his weaknesses. He would later graduate from high school and from Norfolk State University. During the summers, he came back to the choir and worked as an intern.

I treated all of them as my own children, wanting them to have what I didn't growing up—a strong black male in their lives. The choice was not easy. I don't know exactly when it happened, but providing the boys with an alternative to the streets became foremost in my mind. I could see the differences in their upbringing from mine. We started life the same really, just black boys, curious about the ways of survival, with only a mother to answer to. Time and geography were not the only differences, though. I had a village to raise me, constantly encouraging me to get an education to have a better life, one where all things were possible. These children lived in neighborhoods filled with broken-down spirits and a frustrating sense that the weight of the white man crushed all of their positive efforts. The result was a troubling street ethos: get what you can by any way possible. That attitude resulted in lethargy at school, where teachers often didn't care and students cared even less. In order for me to really affect behavior, I needed a school in the European boys choir tradition, where I could provide not just an after-school activity but a quality education, the one sure way to save more lives.

I had already given much of my body and mind to the boys choir. Now I had to give my soul. My singing career, the one thing that propelled me from the cotton fields to the lofty provinces of opera, was placed on hold. This was made less difficult by the lack of opportunities I received to perform. I thought that a beautiful voice could rise above skin color, but race was clearly a factor, and I joined a relatively long line of black singers pounding the pavement for auditions and work. That fire still burns within me, though opera has provided just a little fuel. I remained hopeful, despite history.

Marian Anderson was probably the first black opera singer to receive international acclaim. With her beautiful contralto voice and personal dignity, she did more than any other black singer to break the color line in serious classical music. Paul Robeson and tenor Roland Hayes were probably the first black men to have well-known careers. But in 1939, Anderson became a symbol when the Daughters of the American Revolution refused to let her perform at Constitution Hall in Washington, D.C. Eleanor Roosevelt resigned from the organization in protest and helped arranged for her to sing at the Lincoln Memorial. Seventy-five thousand people attended the open-air Easter Sunday concert and watched tears roll down her cheeks as she sang "America, America." Sixteen years later, she became the first black to sing at the Metropolitan Opera House in its sixty-nine-year history. She appeared as Ulrica in Verdi's *Un Ballo in Maschera*. Past her vocal prime, she sang only a few performances and then retired from opera. She would later explain how she felt about not singing at the Met during her prime: "Years and years ago, I had hoped some day to sing in opera. Later, when some of the things we did in concert gratified us, it did not become a necessity."

I gave it my best shot. I saved up about $5,000 to pay for my debut at Alice Tully Hall. I thought that my performance there would stir up a review or notice, but not much happened as a result. I later landed a role in Scott Joplin's *Treemonisha* on Broadway. That production included Kathleen Battle and Carmen Balthrap, two women who went on to have significant operatic careers. None of the men who performed with me attained such success. Only one, Williard White, left America to have a career in England. Life has not changed much for black males since then. Breaks were rare, and the reason had little to do with talent and everything to do with what was perceived to be socially acceptable. While most audiences have no objection to a white man making love to a black woman on stage, the idea of a black man making up to a white woman aroused too many racial prejudices and stereotypes. I told *The New York*

Times in 1973 about a performance of *Così Fan Tutte* at Brooklyn College: "My first night I played with a black girl, and the audience roared with laughter at everything we did. The next night, I played with a white girl and there was stony silence. Sure, I could have been different the second night, but that different?" George Shirley, a good friend who became a mentor and gave me private voice lessons, had a very good career, performing leading tenor roles at the Metropolitan Opera and major houses across the world for years. More than anyone, he knew the obstacles. "It's male chauvinism," he told *The New York Times.* "Women present no problems to male dominance. Black men do, especially—as some whites think—sexually." Leona Mitchell, another well-known soprano, saw the difference in treatment. "For a black woman it's not necessarily difficult," she told *Ebony* magazine. "But I am very positive that there is a prejudice against black men. Tenors especially—the love-making parts where black men get really close to white women. This disturbs some people."

The other issue that we laughed long and hard about was the so-called reality factor. I remember auditioning for various parts behind a curtain and being told that I had a beautiful voice. They would then ask me to step in front of the curtain. What they saw was a barrel-chested, dark-skinned man with strong African facial features. The next thing I knew, I was being told that I was not "right" for the part. That sort of reasoning was just plain wrong. If singers must look the part that means that an Italian tenor could not be hired as Othello because he doesn't look the part. That means if a company wants to do *Aida,* they can't hire a white soprano because she is not Ethiopian. There had to be some sense of justice. Some white directors argued that only a few blacks had the talent to perform and urged blacks not to let their blackness overshadow their inabilities. They believed that excusing mediocrity with charges of racism was a worse problem. Many of us experienced white directors telling us that we were great singers one day and refusing to let us perform the next. The classic story involved Therman Bailey, a tall, good-looking man who was signed by the Cologne Opera in the mid-seventies. After he arrived in Germany, he told *The New York Times* that he was assigned a large number of roles to prepare for in German. As the weeks went by, he was given more and more roles to learn but never a peformance. He complained and finally worked up the long chain of bureaucracy to the artistic administrator who explained bluntly, "Really, we're not sure how you're going to look onstage." Bailey thundered, "Then why the hell did you hire me? I haven't suddenly changed color."

My voice is fresher now. I have continued to sing even after starting the boys choir, performing recitals once a year at Alice Tully Hall just to keep my name out there. The people who know about my singing are just amazed and sometimes disappointed that I gave it up as a career. Father Williams always told me that I had the sweetest tenor voice since Roland Hayes, and he's probably more upset about my choice than I am. But I was never really convinced that a black man would have the same opportunities as a white man. I do not feel that I am at the boys choir without reason. Part of me believes that it was God's calling. Another part simply wanted to share a variety of music with African-American children and instill a passion for learning and excellence. I wanted our children to know classical music and not be afraid to claim it as their own. In a sense, blacks had segregated themselves from one of the greatest treasures of Western civilization, and I wanted to free the next generation from silly notions that classical music was only for the elite. All of the things that I have learned in pursuit of an operatic career have been helpful to the Boys Choir of Harlem and put the members a notch ahead of everyone else. Most boys choirs are in churches and receive their coaching by musicians not trained as singers. They learn about voice and how to teach voice only as a result of the church asking them to conduct their choir. I am a singer by training, which makes for artistic integrity.

Boy choirs are nothing new and can trace their roots back to the religious ceremonies and rituals in the Middle Kingdom of Egypt around 1500 B.C. The Roman Catholic Church functioned as the fountainhead for the development of choral music and music education. Gregory I, pope from 590 to 604, reorganized the schola cantorum in Rome, which was given the mission to train choir singers. In A.D 597, St. Augustine of Canterbury founded the first song school of first-rate musicians and singers, a tradition that continues today in Europe. Every cathedral and most parish churches have mixed choirs of boys and men. In cathedrals, choristers are usually educated in the choir school attached to the cathedral. The Boys Choir of Harlem is based on those ideals, but the reality of being a poor, black child in Harlem required that our choir be about more than just singing. I would never have the boys' attention or their high level of commitment to the art unless I took care of all their needs.

When I went around the city in the early days trying to persuade people to contribute funds, very few understood my vision. They did not understand how choirs could develop young minds and instill social values. They did not understand the power of music and what it could do, and even today, it's a constant struggle. With the exception of a few art and dance classes, what do public schools offer children who are more creative than athletic? To not use art as an alternative is a crime. In this country, with its frontier mentality, art is considered the dominion of the elite. Many school administrators have few problems eliminating art from core curriculums in public schools across the country. Art is usually the first thing slashed, although it is the one thing that provides a mirror to an individual's soul. Art is where we can really get into the depth of an individual personality, and if we're going to change poor behavior and bad attitudes, then that is where we need to be—inside the heart, where we can instill the system of civility, manners, and precautions perfected over the last several centuries that keep us, for the most part, from killing one another. The brain is easily confused; the heart rarely lies.

The streets have a powerful pull on young impressionable minds, but some of my doubts were erased after our first European tour in 1979. I knew what music could do, but for the first time, the boys saw evidence of things they had not seen. Harlem to Haarlem was a sixteen-day tour, starting in Haarlem, Holland, Harlem's sister city, with stops in Paris and London. Each of the boys kept a diary, and their different observations and thoughts keep me going sixteen years later. The excerpts that follow come from a number of the boys' journals.

December 19

> The day I was told that I had been picked to go on the BCH Harlem to Haarlem tour was the most important day of my life except for the day I was born. . . . I didn't think I would be chosen because sometimes I acted bad in rehearsal, or

don't show up. . . . When we were getting ready for the tour, we had rehearsals every day almost, and I tried my best to do good so I would really make it. . . .

As I boarded the KLM flight, I had a feeling of making a giant step forward as well for all black people. I had never been on a plane before so I was scared. . . . We went up, up, up. . . . If we had gone a few miles higher we would have been in space. On the way over I fell asleep, but before that I tried not to make too much noise because Mr. Turnbull was in the row ahead of me. . . . Finally, after about eight hours, the pilot said, "Fasten your seat belt" like in the movies. . . . I was so excited. I knew I had left the North American continent for the first time ever. . . . It wasn't at all light; you could only see a horizontal kind of rainbow in the sky.

At the airport, we were met by two well-groomed Dutch bus drivers, who were courteous no matter what. . . . We took one of the nicest buses I have ever seen. . . . I remember our old rickety, yellow school bus at home as I get into this streamy line Bovo tour bus. . . . We saw a lot of nice buildings and the streets were very clean. . . . They had bikes all over outside, instead of in their houses. . . . They don't steal bikes in Holland. It's different. . . . It was a pleasure to see our name on big posters on just about every corner. . . . I think almost everybody in Holland knew we were there. . . .

We stayed at one of the most extravagant hotels in Holland called the Sonesta. I knew this tour was going to be hard work right away because it wasn't even three hours before we were all lined up and singing for the Holland press. I have always wanted to be a big brother, and on the tour I had the chance for better or worse. I got two of the most overactive and rebellious little brothers I will ever have the pleasure of not having. They wouldn't fall asleep until the early morning hours, and they didn't get tired until the very end of the trip.

December 20

I saw my first real windmill. What surprised me was that none of the people in Amsterdam wore wooden shoes. We sang for the U.S. ambassador and her board at the Scheveningen Kurhaus, one of the oldest resort hotels. . . . Then we went to a swimming pool that had waves in it that were about four feet high and another one, a little world [whirl] pool. It was fun, but some of us couldn't swim at all. . . . Our dinner at the Lido, now this is one meal I will never forget. This dinner had some beef, rice, and peanut-butter sauce dishes. There were some others, but they were U.D.O.s—unidentified dead objects. That food was so hot, it could burn a hole in a car.

December 21

Because of the very tight and professional-like schedule, there was no room for slow people. . . . If you were slow you could have missed a meal or two. We were lucky enough to visit the Vincent van Gogh art museum, where I learned a few skills to put into my own paintings.

Most of Holland is water. . . . We saw most of Holland, though, through the windows of our buses traveling through rich, middle-class, and slum areas. . . . In Volendam-Edam, the beauty of the little orange-roofed shops and homes, and the old men in their fishing boats, and the children smiling and riding their bikes gave me a totally relaxed feeling that I never could have gotten in New York City.

December 22

Today is my fifteenth birthday and we had an important basketball game at the Van Elden school in the real Haarlem. They seemed to play pretty rough, but we soon adjusted and started to play their type of game. We lost, but we didn't feel too bad about it. If that game was played in New York, we would have won. . . . We learned a new word, "actin-broctin-croktin-conoctin." I don't know what it means, but I'm not Dutch.

We went to the NATO base in Soesterberg. That's the Front Line Fighter Squadron and I must say whosoever dares plan on attacking the U.S. or any of its friendly countries in Europe, I feel sorry for them, for these planes can demolish whatsoever is in their way. . . . There we saw the F-15 Eagle, the fastest plane in the world. We sang for our servicepeople on the air base.

December 23

After the same old breakfast at the Sonesta of jelly, cheese, ham, luncheon meat, pastries, milk, and juice, which they call a continental breakfast, and at first you had to get accustomed to it . . . it was back to the Hague. . . . At the Hague American church they loved us and seemed to applaud for years. Some of us fainted and Mr. Turnbull was mad. . . . Every time someone had to leave because they felt sick, the choir got smaller and smaller. It was terrible. After the concert, the people who were not sick went to a black community. We had some down-home food. . . . That evening we sang at the Koepelzaal, which is one of the unique churches in Amsterdam. There in the center of the domed hall was the first real organ I had ever seen. Its dark brown wood polished to a radiant shine was enhanced by a solid gold figure on the very top. This structure, though *tall and lean, made by man, seemed so natural in the loneliness of the room. . . . The mayor of Amsterdam was there and he met some of the boys. One of the highlights was meeting a prince, the prince of Holland, for the first time in my life. I gave his son my pin of the Big Apple. . . . We became very important ambassadors from the U.S.A. After that performance the audience gave us a standing ovation, and boy did that feel good.*

December 24

The Dutch citizens tried their best to make us feel at home away from home in nice ways. . . . But someone forgot to turn on the heat at St. Bavo. . . . On Christmas Eve I was a little homesick, but my spirits were uplifted when we sang on television. . . . We went to the Hilversun studio for our performance. The choir sang our European hit song, "I Can Sing" on the Tele Bingo *televison show, which for me was one of the biggest thrills.* Tele Bingo *is the biggest show in Holland.*

Every time we got on a bus we knew there was going to be a performance. . . . We got to the packed St. Bavo, all those people packed into that giant cathedral. . . . That organ was the biggest and most beautiful that I had ever seen in my life. The splendor and almost heavenly atmosphere with brass band set aglow by magnificent gold chandeliers and one tiny row of candles through the crowd of seated worshipers singing Christmas carols in Dutch set my heart on fire with thankfulness for being able to be a part of something so nice and beautiful. The most and greatest experience for me was this concert. . . . Everyone had to wear their coats under their robes at St. "Coldo" Bavo.

Spending Christmas Eve in church was a very good feeling because of the mutual love that existed that night. The

audience was alive with pleasure. After the concert was
over, we all went into a back room to celebrate with cookies
and hot chocolate. . . . On our bus back to the Sonesta we
got all the good music from stateside. . . . We were singing
and dancing to "Rapper's Delight" four times back to back.
The bus was shaking, and it shook all the way back to the
hotel.

December 25

We finally had time on Christmas day to explore the neigh-
borhood around the Sonesta and the pinball gallery and to
do some of the shopping. I got souvenirs and presents for
my family. That evening we had a party in the Sonesta's
disco, where we exchanged gifts and were then surprised
by the presentation of some foxy ladies from the black com-
munity in Holland. They would dance with us and play
games with us. So the party was for six hours. Wow did we
have fun. I stayed up all night to pack my clothes and get
ready for the trip to Paris the next morning.

December 26

The trip from Holland was about 10 hrs . . . 11 hrs . . . 12
hrs . . . 13 hrs . . . by bus. That morning everyone was
tired. As we arrived in Paris, I had the feeling of sleeping
in another hotel, but instead, we arrived at an orphanage
where we made modifications for our stay. In the orphan-
age all the boys felt a sorrow experience. It was probably
because they felt homesick. For me it was an enjoyable ex-
perience because I felt I was really living a French life some-
what different than an American life. . . . We had to sleep
the best way we could.

December 27

It was a very busy country. . . . We went to the Eiffel Tower and we saw the original Statue of Liberty. . . . Paris was where we learned about the trains and buses. On the train there is a machine which you put a card in and wait till a light comes on and just walk through. The train doors are different, too. They don't open by a conductor. You have to push up on the lock and the door will open.

December 28

This performance lasted one hour in length. . . . It was at the Salle de Fete at the 6th Arrondissement. . . . We had to walk to the concert, but they sent some beat-up old ambulance to pick up the instruments. . . . At the rooming house, there are hard pillow fights, hard fights also. Mr. T tore some butts up with his belt. . . . It was kind of funny.

December 30

Our concerts in Paris were just as moving as in Holland. We sang at the infamous Notre Dame Cathedral. . . . Unfortunately we didn't see the hunchback, but it was still exciting. . . . There was the organ I call the Phantom Organ because I never saw it, only its outline under dark lights. I only heard the sound of it as it added mystery and aged beauty. . . . We sang our best. It was our best concert. . . . Mr. Turnbull told us to let it all out and we did. . . . I felt glowing with pride and honor to be, more than likely, in the first black group to sing there from our country and maybe even the world. What surprised me the most was they loved the way we were singing. We receive many standing ovations. . . . We sang so good that people didn't want to leave. I must admit that Mr. Turnbull sang well, too. They also demanded many encores, which made us feel very good and very wanted.

We had a little jerk for a bus driver. He was a little dimbo. He had no consideration at all. Again we sang at St. Germain des Pres. They loved us. We were terrific. I went out that night with Mrs. Brown and Charles for a taste of French pizza, to our regret, but in spite of pizzas we enjoyed the laughter of trying to order not understanding or speaking any French, which was also to the amusement of the French people at the table next to us.

December 31

The French were very lively and friendly by hugging and kissing to welcome the new year. Later we were a part of the love and happiness expressed by the Parisians on the Champs-Elyssees [sic] by being held up in traffic with people who were all out to have a good time.

January 1

We sang at a hospital for mentally and physically disrupted children. That was a very nice performance. . . . Our last concert in Paris was sung for senior citizens.

As we left Paris I looked back at the place where I slept and I said to myself that I will never forget the place that I called home for six days because I knew somebody else gave it up for us. All in all, France is artistically delicious.

January 2

We left Paris at 6:40 A.M. We were going to England. We took a bus, a boat, and then another bus. The first bus ride took four hours, the boat eight hours. We boarded another bus and I said here we go again, and this bus took seven hours. It was hard being locked up in a bus for these long rides. I especially loved the warm, white Lincoln Cathedral with its organ that separated the cathedral into churches. This old English organ, encased in a white stone monument complete with television cameras for viewing the church, rang out the songs, as the choir proudly sang to the filled cathedral. . . . I felt so at one with the surroundings and proud to be part of such beauty. Lincoln Cathedral was very big. It had about four sections and graves all around the place. The large audience from the small community welcomed us gracefully. We spent the night in a girls' college which was cold and scary. Me and my friend Scot was so scared we slept together.

January 3

In the morning, we rode the bus for a long time until we made a couple of stops to use the restroom and then right back on the bus again. Our last day of the tour, we were looking forward to this day for a long time and our last performance at St. Paul's is a good one. We did very well . . . we sang our hearts out. . . . We weren't too well received at St. Paul Cathedral . . . the people were dead. There was no life in them. I was stunned by the golden towering ceilings and the tombs of people like Florence Nightingale in the basement. It was our last day in music.

After this we got the Harry and Harry tour of London and Westminster. London wouldn't have been much fun without Harry Beaury and Harry the English bus driver who looked like something right out of the movies, short and weighing something like 300 pounds and had a bad English accent. . . . The tour guide asked us who was England's biggest traitor. No one knew. He says George Washington. . . . I saw Big Ben. We saw the entrance to Buckingham Palace and the entrance to Scotland Yard. . . .

Then after that, we took a ship back to Hoek van Hol-
land. . . . This boat ride is an experience itself. . . . On the
ship three quarters of the choir got sick. Dr. Mahon didn't
know which way to turn. If I didn't laugh so much, I
wouldn't have got sick.

January 4

We managed to reach Holland in one piece and go to the
airport for the glorious ride home. . . . Finally we were in
the air on the KLM Airlines. I could not wait until I got back
home. We got home that same day later that night. . . . I
was looking very hard until I seen my mother. I jumped so
high that everyone looked at me. I ran to my mother. She
grabbed me so hard that I was in a 5 second shock. When I
arrived home the first thing I did was eat some soul food—
McDonald's.

Europe, one day I will return. It was a cultural exchange
I will never forget, yet it was an exhausting trip, but no one
said it would be easy. I got the chance to do something I
love to do, sing. For me, the tour was, to sum it up, joy,
hard work, fun, gratitude, love, friendship, and respect . . .
and I hope I can stay in the choir for seven more years and
even more I want to earn my scholarship in music.

More than anything, the European tour put the choir on
the map. They had traveled halfway around the world, seen
things that many of their parents had only read about. The
New York Daily News proclaimed in one headline: THE NEW
HARLEM GLOBE TROTTERS. We received great reviews. C'EST MAG-
NIFIQUE, screamed one French newspaper. "The voices of
the children are very beautiful," wrote *Le Matin.* "An ad-
venture in extraordinary music. . . . We understand why
these young artists are called 'Children of the Sun,' " wrote

Classique Paris, From Harlem to Haarlem: Story of a Choirboy, the WABC television program detailing the life of one of our boys during the trip, won an Emmy Award for best children's programming. The boys received confirmation that they were on the right track. I saw how hard the boys were willing to work to achieve excellence onstage and receive applause and standing ovations. They felt wanted. They felt valuable. They saw the reward for their efforts.

Everything was coming together. My style of music teaching was a combination of Herticene Jones and Pops: discipline and polish. The boys were eager, and I used their desire to become stars as a carrot, dangling international tours and performances in front of them until they worked and worked and worked. The stick was being left behind. But in order to get the most of these children, I needed to create a environment similiar to the one behind the gates at Tougaloo, one that was safe, secure, and nurturing. I lacked one critical piece—counseling.

Frank Jones solved that problem in September 1980. He had been working as a counselor with a social agency in New York City, and I had met him through another counselor who was working part-time at the choir. Jones knew little of the Boys Choir of Harlem, but was intrigued with the idea of establishing a counseling service at an arts organization. Our meeting in the common room at the Church of the Intercession provided answers for me and for him. I told him that children came here every day with emotional and social baggage shared by many kids growing up in New York City. The message struck a chord in Frank. He, too, had grown up in the city and knew what it was like trying to balance leading the life of a child with the reality of living amid a slew of social imperfections and decay. Urban life had worsened from the time Frank was a child in the sixties, and it was clear to him, almost immediately, that we needed a counseling service.

One of the initial problems was determining just how the service would function within the framework of a performing arts group. The counseling unit could not become a competitor with the artistic program; it really had to be a supportive element, capable of adapting to whatever changes were happening with the artistic activities. Jones's background seemed to enable him to fit right in with what I had envisioned. He knew how to establish an environment for counseling. In his mind, there was no place that was inappropriate. There are some counseling approaches that can only happen in a predisposed, prearranged situation. There are some people who don't have the flexibility within their own training to be able to say, "Well, maybe it could work, even if it doesn't have a desk or an office." Jones's training allowed him to say, "Counseling can happen even if you are sitting on top of the George Washington Bridge."

Jones accepted the job the next week and quickly established himself among the boys. He was hard not to notice. Handsome and articulate, he stood about six feet tall and had a powerfully built body. The boys would later call him Diesel. Jones grew up across the river in Long Branch, New Jersey. He ran track and played basketball in high school, and his name back then was synonomous with striving to be a champion. His teenage friends, already drinking and smoking, still respected and cheered him during meets or back on the corner. Jones went on to Central State University in Ohio, then received a graduate degree in psychology from the University of Minnesota. He came back to New York City after working for a while in Minnesota and Chicago. He wanted to work in New York City because he felt the intensity of the problems that he wanted to deal with existed here in abundance.

Jones was also a performer and understood the almost unbridled desire by teenagers to become big-time stars making big-time money. He grew up on Motown and the Temptations, Smokey Robinson, and Marvin Gaye, and when he was in high school, he held auditions in his mother's house for a little rhythm and blues band he had started. He still had his own band when he started working at the Boys Choir, the Twilights, which played at clubs in the New York City area. Frank was the lead singer and producer. He was also the only one with a full-time job. Some of the musicians in the band got caught up in the cocaine scene, later graduating to prison. The band fizzled. Jones was walking a thin line between doing something legitimate with the Boys Choir of Harlem and trying to make it as a singer, slipping and sliding in a business filled with con artists and predators. He had integrity, though, and didn't have to do anything unseemly to make a buck.

There were about forty children in the choir when Jones opened his office in the basement of the Church of the Intercession. He started on September 28, and the mood of the choristers was gloomy. That summer, one of the first boys to join, Mervin Lewis, had drowned at Rockaway Beach. I remember flying back from California, where I was attending a seminar on boys choirs, to attend the funeral. Mervin was a great kid and had rejoined the choir after his mother, a member of Ephesus Church, pulled him out. She was one of the parents who disagreed with changing the name to include Harlem. His best friend was another choir member, Leroy Williams, who would later become a New York City police officer. Both of them lived in the Bronx, and Williams would often ride his bicycle to Lewis's apartment. They were inseparable. "We were so close; I don't have a best friend now," Williams told me. They attended school together and joined the choir together. They played basketball together and double-dated together. They called the two or three strands of peach fuzz their "mustafas." They also started a singing group, the Gospel Specials, together.

The beach was supposed to have been a big party that day. Two years earlier, Lewis had met a house full of sisters, all gorgeous, as Williams tells it. The girls came to their concerts and the boys took them to movies and ice cream stores. They were one big group. They planned the beach party for weeks. They were going to party from sunup to sundown, swimming, barbecuing. They were even going to have one of those bonfires. The day finally came. They rode the subway out to Coney Island beach in Brooklyn. Lewis wasn't worried that he couldn't swim. "I won't drown," he told Williams, "because I can float. You will be tired from doing all of that swimming." None of them checked the weather report. If they had, they would have known that a tropical storm was brewing. The waves grew larger and larger as they frolicked in the water. A lifeguard blew his whistle, signaling the swimmers to go ashore, but the group stayed in, yelling, screaming, having fun. All of a sudden, Williams recalled, a humongous wave, building for miles, crashed ashore, knocking the party down and underwater. Everybody came up after a minute or so. Except Mervin. Williams said everyone simply waited for him to surface. He doesn't remember whether he went home during the wait or not. Either way, Lewis didn't wash ashore for four days.

From his office, Jones could watch the kids walk through the hallway until they reached the game room, where they waited for rehearsals to begin. Everyone was sullen and sad; the whole atmosphere was one of melancholy. The choir was a close-knit group, their bond made tighter after their European tour the year before. Jones thought that maybe the listlessness was just the temperament of the children. He knew that many of them had grown up in the church, and he figured they were a little laid-back.

Jones did some probing. As he began to listen, he learned about the drowning and how it was almost sacrilegious to laugh. The choir was in mourning. It took some time, probably about three months, before Lewis's death no longer dominated the atmosphere. It was difficult for the children to really adjust to that loss. "I felt sorry for Mr. Jones," Williams said. "He had to come in and deal with that. And really, nobody really wanted to talk about it, and Jones wanted people to talk about it. We were boys becoming men, and back in that day, there wasn't no Oprah; you weren't supposed to be sensitive. Coming back for those first few rehearsals was tough because Mervin wasn't there. You know, you figuring nobody's supposed to die at fifteen, you know what I mean? You got your whole life ahead of you." One of Jones's first missions, then, was trying to restore the delicate equilibrium in the group. We had to convince the children that it was all right to be productive again, that it was all right to be concerned about the here and now, and that it was all right to think about having fun again. It was almost as if they had to get permission to start living again. As a trained social worker, Jones wanted to tell them, rather bluntly, that Lewis was dead, and it was time for them to move on. But he didn't and instead listened to what they had to say and allowed them to figure out their own way of dealing with the loss of one of their friends.

∞

That approach became the catalyst for a startling discovery about young black males, especially young teenagers: unless they had been accustomed to having a male figure around the house, talking to an adult male was unnecessary. They had survived without one from an early age and really didn't see the need. Jones changed all of that. The boys were receptive, and it was almost a revelation for some of them that they could in fact use a male figure in their lives, someone to whom they could be sensitive and show their weaknesses. They learned that it was all right to unravel and unveil things that were almost like personal secrets. We realized that most of these kids never had anyone, not a counselor in their school or churches, who they could relate to and discuss their lives and feelings with. All they had were adults telling them what they should not do or should not feel. No one was telling them what they could do or feel. We tried to give the children perspective, not formulas or John Wayne–type solutions like "suck it up, be a man." Children, especially black boys, have been barraged with such clichés, which may work in the movies but have little power helping children regain a sense of confidence after having a negative experience of one kind or another. Each of the boys had his own personality and abilities. Some required very little in terms of guidance; others were in either Frank's or my office constantly. We had all types and encountered all kinds of situations. In listening to the boys and their parents, it was becoming increasingly clear that we needed to have our own school, one where the values of discipline and hard work could be reinforced throughout the day.

Luke "Tiny" Drew was a very talented kid. He came from P.S. 28 to an audition, and I was struck by his lovely voice. He was a slim little guy, very personable. People loved to talk with him after a performance. I remember having to scold him for having a pillow fight during the European tour. Part of the reason that he liked the choir so much was that he could be onstage, showing off his talents. He and his brothers had already had bit parts in the movie *The Wiz.* They also had earned a small part in the Big Apple Circus. Performing was very exciting to him. He had a very limber body and had taken some classes at the Dance Theatre of Harlem. During performances back then, we had an act where some of the kids would tumble and do flips onstage. That period was interesting because black kids across the country were discovering their bodies and doing what they called "electrified dances." They were simply using their innate and natural abilities. Without any formal training, they could look at a dance on television, then go out and do it. Tiny was one those kids.

Tiny was enterprising and unafraid. No one would be surprised to see Tiny and a few of his boys anywhere in New York City at any time of day or night. His father worked as a subway conductor, which was considered a good job because it had benefits such as health insurance and a pension. But he also had a heavy drinking problem and was the type of parent who believed that as long as his son wasn't dead or behind bars, he was doing a good job. By all accounts, he was failing. Tiny's mother was very sickly and exerted little influence over any of her nine children, leaving them pretty much on their own. At least two of his four older brothers were in jail by the time he started singing with the choir, and as time went on, the others joined them. They remained Tiny's heroes, though. He believed that his brothers were misunderstood and that their incarcerations, based on drug convictions, were unjustified.

He couldn't wait for them to finish serving their time because, in a sense, he wanted to be just like them.

Tiny grew up near 152nd Street and Amsterdam Avenue, an area laden with drugs. People were afraid to come out of their apartments at night because of frequent shoot-outs. Tiny was a daredevil and had hobbies like martial arts. He always talked about joining the army. But going into the army also meant being able to kill, having enough guts to kill, being able to take pain and hardship. Tiny always wanted to test himself, and because he was skinny and considered small, he got into frequent fights with teen-agers sometimes three times his size. He knew he had strength and guts. Sometimes, he would win, sometimes lose. He was always proud to show off his latest scar. It was almost like a death wish, and I was afraid for him because he had so much to prove, and I just knew that he would end up dead. A few years after the European tour, Tiny dropped out of the choir. He thought that he had outgrown it. Even though he no longer wanted to be a part of the choir, we still supported him. We never prevented young men from doing what they wanted to do, and in a sense, developing the ability to think and act for oneself is arguably our most important goal. We helped him get into an alternative high school in New York City, but after a year, he dropped out of that, too. He just wasn't interested in sitting down in a classroom anymore; he wanted to be out among the real people, the men and women in the military. He joined the army and was stationed in Pennsylvania.

At least Tiny had some get-up-and-go. At the other end of the spectrum was Jonathon Grant. He started when the choir was at Ephesus Church, and he is still with us as an alumnus. I remember when his father, a deacon at the church, came up to me and asked if I could get his son into the choir. He started when he was about eight years old. His parents were very supportive. The lived in the projects on the east side of Harlem. They had two children and lavished more attention on their son than on their daughter, who received little. Every time I talked to the parents, it was Jonathon this, or Jonathon that. Even at an early age Jonathon was very preoccupied with what other people thought. He never had drive; he just did what he had to do.

He never took anything really seriously. He didn't do that well academically. He was a slow learner and went to the Adventist Academy, then to the Adventist High School, Northeastern Academy, and then off to Oakwood College, where he messed up, didn't study, rented cars, and played the girls. His parents finally stopped sending money for tuition, so he had to come back home. He started going to the Borough of Manhattan Community College, and he came back to sing tenor and bass with the choir. He has always been very loyal to the Boys Choir of Harlem. He has a very good talent and an extraordinarily good ear. He has a pretty voice, but his lack of drive precludes him from rising above the pack. In all the years that he has been associated with the choir, he has never asked to have a solo. He would never ask for voice lessons to improve himself. I tried encouraging him to do different things, and even hired him as a teacher at the choir. Through many one-on-ones, I have tried to encourage him to use his standing as a symbol of what a person can become if in fact they use all the supports that the BCH has to offer. He simply nods his head, saying, "Yes, yes, yes, yes," but then goes right back to his life of complacency.

* * *

More than any other case, the story of Muhammad and Hassan Worthy demonstrated to me that the public schools were not only underpreparing minority children but also affecting their outlook on life, often for the worse. Family dynamics played a strong role as well, but something happened to a significant portion of children once they started attending classes. They would come in energetic and return listless. Such was the case with the Worthy brothers. They came from P.S. 28 on the corner of 155th. They were two very nice kids when I first met them. Both of them had wonderful attitudes and were proud of the fact that they were Muslims. They would often tell people that they didn't eat pork. Sometimes they said it unnecessarily, just to express what and who they were. They were very interested in the music and both had very pretty treble voices. They auditioned for the choir and were accepted by the time they were in elementary school. They were ready to go to the first summer camp, and their mother had paid $100 to hold their spots. But then they discovered that both of them had a trace tuberculosis and couldn't attend. Once that happened, they never came back to the choir. For many years I would see them walking on the streets, and they would say hello. Sometimes they would be with their mother, and all of them were very cordial. The next thing I knew, they were in high school and wanted to be a part of the choir.

They seemed very different children then. When they first auditioned, Muhammad and Hassan were very competitive with one another; Hassan had always been considered by his teachers to be the more stable of the two. Hassan was actually the first person I chose; Muhammad, the older of the two, came to the audition simply because his younger brother needed someone to bring him there.

Muhammad was not without talent but was inconsistent and didn't have the natural ability of his brother. Both of them were very dark-skinned and received a lot of teasing. As a result, they stuck pretty close together at school and had very low opinions of themselves. They didn't feel attractive, something that especially affected Muhammad. He knew the significance of all the negative comments. Hassan brushed them off because he wasn't that concerned with what people thought about him.

Their parents had separated when they were young. Their father was stern and domineering; the mother was very much afraid. She decided to leave because the father had actually required his sons to drop out of the BCH, despite his wife's desire for them to remain in the choir. He considered some of the music that we were singing to be religious and aligned with Christianity, not Islam. She eventually left him for good, and Frank recalls seeing her and her children one day walking along the 155th Street Bridge in the Bronx pushing a shopping cart filled with their belongings. She came to the BCH the next day and promptly told Frank that she had left her husband and was going to raise her children by herself. She didn't want to go on welfare, she told Frank, and would find a job. She also wanted them to have a positive alternative and asked if they could rejoin the choir.

When they came back, Muhammad was already starting his freshman year of high school. Hassan was at junior high school; not only had he gotten involved with a group of kids who weren't doing anything, he was turning into a wanderer. He would not go into the school building. He would leave the house and just wander the streets. He often talked of suicide. Muhammad, on the other hand, was becoming a recluse. He was not leaving the house. The mother simply kept this secret to herself. She did not know that her children really needed psychiatric care.

Muhammad never developed a trust in people, despite our efforts. He began to live a fantasy about completing school and going on to college when in fact he was not earning his high school credits. Being in the BCH meant a lot to him because it was one of the few activities where he was achieving something; he had opportunities to go on tour, which helped him, and he even got high school credit for it. But he gradually turned inward again, and his mother felt there was little that she could do to get him out of the house and socialize. He was always late for rehearsals. He never came anywhere near on time. Occasionally he was more than an hour late. Muhammad was intelligent, but he was incapable of assessing himself realistically. He thought he was perfect and didn't need to develop anymore.

Hassan, by contrast, started hanging out with a group of people who had similar conditions and problems. He couldn't hang around achievers because deep down he felt inferior. He knew that he had the intellect and ability to be with that group of people, but he didn't want to earn his place. I always had the sense that both of them didn't feel that they had to work for anything. And yet they wanted the reward of going on tour. Both of them stopped coming to practice, even though we had told them repeatedly that they were still welcome. But they had to meet us at least halfway, which they never did.

There always seemed to be a crisis. Before Frank Jones started working with the choir, I didn't have anyone to dedicate adequate time to the children's problems. Sometimes I ended up just having to cross my fingers and praying that everything would work out. But many of the kids were dropping out for a variety of reasons. When Frank came along, he intervened and developed ways for the Boys Choir of Harlem to help. He would talk with parents and assure them that the choir would keep their child busy while they straightened out their difficulties. Seemingly overnight we went from being a choir only to a choir with a child-care component. That required interaction, if not face-to-face then certainly over the telephone, with parents on a regular basis. We started monitoring school attendance and behavior, and Jones and I would talk almost every day about the lives of our charges.

There were some children whose situations were definitely problematic. Without the necessary resources, I had no other choice but to ask the most troublesome to leave. By now I had realized that I could not save every child. We had expanded the choir to include children from the community, not just members of the Ephesus or Intercession churches. Many of these kids didn't have church backgrounds and needed to have an extra effort to keep them involved. They had usually heard about the choir through word of mouth, or they had a friend or relative in the choir. There wasn't a set pattern back then for auditions. As time went on, we couldn't depend on happenstance. We needed to have trebles—the backbone of any boys choir—but the pool was limited. I finally established a relationship with P.S. 28. We needed to have between fifteen and twenty young men training as trebles. The principal there loved the idea and agreed to open his school gym at 7:30 A.M. so that we could hold rehearsals there. These children were in the training phase, so they didn't attend the regular afternoon rehearsals. In the old days, everyone just rehearsed together. By now, we had developed a level of sophistication, and mixing the trained boys with the untrained generated too many disruptions and too much loss of time. The third graders had to be motivated enough to be in school early in the morning twice a week. There were initially ten guys in our very first tryouts. From there, they graduated to the summer training program.

The summer camps proved vital to providing thorough counseling and music training. We really worked on technique, vocal drills, and breathing exercises with the same intensity as basketball players at summer camp. We worked four hours in the morning, three hours in the afternoon, and usually a few hours after dinner. There was time for fun, but the camps were mostly about work. The counseling was equally as important. Jones had a nondirective philosophy, meaning that instead of a counselor telling a person what to do, the counselor would give a person choices, and that person would choose whichever one he wanted. But Jones realized that this approach worked best when counselors were in a come-and-go relationship with people. Counseling the boys was a different matter. We took on the responsibility of monitoring their behavior and teaching them at critical periods in their lives. We had to be more directive. We had to tell people what we wanted and what we needed to see happen in their lives. Jones had been very comfortable with the nondirective approach; it didn't really require as much emotionally. It was like saying, "Okay, I told you what you can do. If you want to do it, fine. If you don't listen, I'm going home. It doesn't matter to me. I'll be here on Monday; tell me about it."

We wanted a certain outcome from the people receiving our counseling. The molding and strategies that we used simply to involve the person in the very beginning became a lot different. It required more thought and a lot more care. We had to think about things in stages. Before it was sort of like one great big experience. Now we went in stages: first, I learned their names; next, I learned their strengths and weaknesses, then some of the things that were hidden. At that point, we were ready to change some of the stuff that didn't work and teach some skills that did. We are at our best when we see the children develop through all of the stages. That is why it is important to have them live away at camp so we can see all the layers unfold. We need to determine whether a child is high-risk or able to learn the values of the choir.

We launched our first national tour in 1983. With the exception of Europe, most of our performances had been local and did not require overnight stays. We couldn't afford to pay for food and lodging on the meager fees we received, and we really couldn't pass along the costs to the parents. Word had started spreading about our unique sound throughout the city. Requests from churches in Queens, Brooklyn, and the Bronx were frequent. We had a little yellow school bus, owned by a Spanish lady, that broke down constantly, leaving us stranded for a while until a mechanic arrived and fixed whatever was wrong. Miraculously, we never missed a performance, but it was clear that we needed another bus to travel cross-country. The tour was seventeen days, and the fees were so low that we had to string together about twenty performances, literally to sing for our dinner. I had hired a manager to find the gigs and make all the arrangements. To make sure the children kept up with their schoolwork, Frank Jones called their teachers and received all of their students' course work and assignments.

The lowest bidder for the bus contract was an older gentleman from Queens. He claimed to have a bus, and he did have one, but it suffered from all sorts of maladies. In order to start the bus, he had to take a stick, an old branch from a tree, lift up the engine cover, and wiggle the stick somewhere in the engine until he heard a click. I guess it was comparable to hot-wiring a car. When I first saw Dilliard Boone, our first general manager, holding up the engine hood, I didn't think anything of it. We were well on the road when Jones and Boone explained the procedure to me, but by then it was too late. And the engine always started, so there was no real problem. The driver's keyless ignition was certainly not on his bid. We drove from New York straight to St. Louis. Somewhere near Indiana, we faced a torrential downpour. It was about 3 A.M., and everyone was asleep, except Jones and the bus driver. As Jones tells it, sheets of water cascaded off the front windshield. Many other drivers had pulled off to the side of the road, but not ours. He was cruising along at eighty-five miles per hour, unworried. He'd hit a bump in the road, and the bus seemed to take flight, skimming what Frank said appeared to be waves like a surfboard. Frank recalled looking out of the window and asking himself, "Are we going to make it?" We made it, and from that point on, the boys dubbed the driver DOT—Director of Transportation.

He was a tall, heavyset man, a nice brother who had a little street in him. At the gas station, for instance, he had figured out a way to squeeze a few extra gallons for free. He would pull the bus in front of where the attendant was stationed and start pumping the gas. He would then ask Jones to take the hose as he held the thin wire attached to the pump and hose. Somehow, that stopped the register from counting the gallons. He was great to the kids, always telling them stories about staying in school and making the right decisions. He also was willing to help out with loading and unloading musical equipment. He worked with the choir for about three years, when we agreed that he was no longer capable of meeting our needs. He knew it and we knew it. The Boys Choir of Harlem was quickly becoming a nationally known group.

Of Morals and Young Men

IN A SENSE, I have taken on what some of the Great Society programs had started in the sixties: trying to balance the social gaps in children created by the legacy of slavery and the collision of two of America's most treasured ideals: the democratic notion of equal rights and the capitalist reality of unequal incomes. The bridge between the two is society's loosely defined theory of upward mobility. In theory, everyone is able to transcend environment and move up the social ladder, their skills and competence rewarded by the marketplace. The first step is establishing a sense of purpose, and if the children don't have it when they arrived at the Boys Choir of Harlem, they certainly learn quickly.

I had also taken on the ancient challenge of providing an education that connects matters of the heart with matters of the intellect. Aristotle wrote:

> In modern times there are opposing views about the practice of education. There is no general agreement about

what the young should learn either in relation to virtue or in relation to the best in life; nor is it clear whether their education ought to be directed more towards the intellect than towards the character of the soul. The problem has been complicated by what we see before our eyes, and it is not certain whether training should be directed at things useful in life, or at those conducive to virtue, or nonessentials. And there is no agreement as to what in fact does tend towards virtue. Men do not prize most highly the same virtue, so naturally they differ also about the proper training for it.

Reading, writing, and arithmetic are subjects taught in virtually every school in America with varying degrees of success. Teaching children morals, however, is complicated (the questions of whose values and how are constant) and viewed by some as "mushy" and irrelevant. Nothing could be further from the truth. At the Boys Choir of Harlem, we are very much interested in a child's academic performance and stress that a B average must be maintained in order to travel with the performing choir. Academics and standardized test scores, however, are only a part of a child's social development. We are much more interested in the development of the whole child, the stuff that is immeasurable to a certain degree. In order to accomplish our goal of developing children of character, we established an environment in which books and character play equal roles. A child's behavior then, whether or not he has acted as a good citizen, also plays a vital role in determining whether he can travel with the choir.

It is the combination of both—intellect and heart—that prevents children from falling into the human scrap heap of no marketable skills, unemployment, drug and alcohol abuse, and illegal behavior. Our method is at once simple and complicated. We establish a positive environment for children to develop all of their skills. Once the heart is safe, the mind follows. We help children determine what is right and what is wrong. The relationship between students and teachers is one of kinship, where communication is a two-way street. Each child is different and brings a different set of challenges. It is up to the individual teacher, then, to discover the individual core of each and every child. The discovery process takes time.

As noted educator Theodore Sizer writes in *Horace's Compromise*, high schools exist not merely to subject the pupils to brute training—memorizing geometry theorems, learning how to mend an axle, reciting a passage from *Macbeth*—but to develop their powers of thought, of taste, and of judgment.

> Such undertakings cannot be factory-wrought, for young people grow in idiosyncratic, variable ways, often unpredictably. Good teachers are essential to nourish this growth. . . . It is their judgment and inspiration that can help young persons. No "system" or "school site leadership," no "treatment" or "intervention," no "innovative program," "approved textbook," or "curriculum guide" can overcome their influence, for good or ill. Learning is a humane process, and young humans look to those human elders with whom they are in daily contact for standards, for help, and as models.

The cookie-cutter approach does not work when it comes to imparting values. Though there are some universal characteristics among children throughout the world, their environment, language, and situations are different. Our specific method of teaching in Harlem may not work in Des Moines, Iowa, but the general methods are the same. Establishing trust between teacher and student is paramount to success. Trust is established by demonstrating a genuine concern for a child's well-being. That means talking with a child and actually listening to him or her. Most children have something that they do of which they are proud. Sometimes it's coloring or working with clay. Or it might be building model cars. The children often hold their interests a secret. All it takes is a simple question from a teacher: "What do you like doing?" If the child answers he likes to draw, ask him to bring his work in. It's amazing to see what children are proud of, and praise usually comes naturally.

From that point on, a bond has been established. The student sees that the teacher is interested in him as a person, not just as some body sitting in a class. The teacher sees that the child is capable of a variety of skills— attention to detail, ability to complete a task, and courage to share a secret with an adult. It's the little things upon which the larger things are built. During an audition, for example, if a child comes up to me, I am impressed. It shows me that he is not afraid of adults and has a certain belief in himself. When a teacher tells me that a child is unable to learn, it suggests that the teacher has not pushed the right buttons, not asked the right questions to untap the curiosity that lies in every child. It also suggests that the teacher may think the child does not have an untapped potential and is unworthy of teaching.

Imparting moral and intellectual virtues is a responsibility left largely to public schools, and more specifically, to the adults, mostly teachers, who work in those schools. Children determine what is important by gauging the behavior of the adults in their lives. Gerald Grant writes in *The World We Created at Hamilton High*: "The adults epitomize some version of character to pupils—by ignoring or responding to incidents of racism in the classroom or hallway, by the manner in which they answer a child's earnest inquiry, by the respect they show for the qualities of intellect, by the agreements they make about what behavior will not be tolerated as well as what actions will be honored." In this debate on virtues, creating the right environment is crucial.

Punctuality was—and still is—the first lesson. In the early eighties, rehearsals began at 4 P.M. at the Church of the Intercession. The older boys already knew to be on time. Some of them probably had suffered the embarrassment of coming late to rehearsal in the past; they usually came to the vestibule, where we kept a sign-in sheet and posted rehearsal schedules, about forty-five minutes early. It was important to read the schedules back then. Access to rehearsal halls changed frequently. Sometimes the sopranos and altos rehearsed in the gymnasium; other times they rehearsed in the Guild Room. For the first two weeks, new choir members had not yet learned the ropes and came to rehearsal when they saw fit. "You are early for tomorrow's rehearsal," I would thunder. "I know you are not coming into my class at this hour of the day." If the straggling student offered any kind of excuse, I demanded that he tell the entire class. After all, his disruption cost them precious time; ultimately, he owed them an apology, and more important, a commitment to arrive on time in the future. The other students usually snickered—some even laughed aloud—as the tardy one concocted some sort of explanation. After about the third week and a few more outbursts from me, any students not in their seats at 4 P.M.

sharp had called before class to let me know that they were not going to be there.

Public humiliation was a great motivator, and nothing was too small to launch into a larger lesson on life. If a child asked to be excused to use the bathroom only ten minutes after rehearsal had begun, I would tell the boy and the class about the word "preparation" and how they had to plan things in their lives. Punctuality and preparation are relatively simple things, but unless an issue is made of them, kids have no idea how important they are in achieving success. Learning music demands discipline. It takes at least a year for untrained singers to learn not only vocal technique but also the basic language of music. It also takes them a while to understand how to use their bodies. They must know what I mean when I ask for a sigh or for tallness of their soft palate. They need to learn how to breathe correctly and use their diaphragms properly. They need to know the correct posture to get the most from their bodies.

We are building voices. They develop over time, much like any athlete's muscles. The vocal cords are muscles, which must be strengthened and exercised. It's the same process as a basketball player learning how to dribble, and it doesn't come naturally in all cases. Children are born with certain talents and have different degrees of ability. Each is born with a certain set of vocal cords and a certain head structure. Some voices are better than others; all can be developed. Our approach to teaching voice is different from the traditional English style. We encourage boys, for instance, to keep singing through their voice change. Under the traditional style, those boys are shunted aside, no longer needed by the choir.

During this learning process, we observe the children to determine whether they have short attention spans or not, whether they have the discipline to stick with what is often difficult, and whether they simply want the fame without the effort. Counseling sessions support our direct observations. We ask children about the ups and downs of their families, if they have had any major illnesses or injuries. In subsequent talks with a child's parents, we try to learn whether the child has any learning disabilities that might affect their judgment or reasoning skills and whether they have been involved in situations that have caused emotional trauma. These profiles become increasingly important once children are ready to perform on tour. Our tours can last for three weeks at a time, and we are relying on the sensibility of a child to act and behave accordingly. I am not reluctant to remove a child from the organization if I believe I cannot supervise him. I must be able to do that. We have had experiences with very emotionally disturbed children. Not everyone who comes here can take full advantage of what we have to offer. We don't have the resources or the time—especially considering the vast numbers of children deemed unworthy in mainstream society who have needs that we can meet.

Once the children know the importance of arriving on time, the next lesson is increasing their attention spans and developing their ability to stand still for long periods of time. In order to teach children how to sing, we show them how to stand with their feet in the right place—spread about hip-width apart with one foot slightly in front of the other—their backs straight and chests up. Almost immediately, we are socializing the children, helping them eliminate their youthful tendencies to slouch and lean. That's part of the choir's magical abilities: it's as if they're learning to sing and hold their heads pridefully upright at the same time. Fourth graders usually arrive here with short attention spans. For the most part, they have not been challenged either at home or at school. They have been given mimeograph sheets by day and television at night. They are bored. We push them. We talk about paying attention as an important part of character development, something to be proud of. We make it interesting. We play games. We have them line up and stare at something on the wall. I'll go around the room, pretending I don't notice any of them: if I catch someone taking their eyes off the spot, that person has to sit down. It's fun for them and improves their level of concentration. Initially, the exercises are thirty minutes longer than the kids can stand. We push and push and push until their times increase. It's not all fun and is often arduous. But after a few years of training, they can go for several hours, if needed, standing in concert position rehearsing a song. Teachers must push in order to improve their students. The only limitations on our children are the limitations of the teachers.

We don't place all of the blame on children for their inabilities. If a child is not reading at the end of a school year, for instance, the question is not what is wrong with the child but rather what is wrong with the teacher's approach. Part of the reason that parents put their children's development in our hands is that we believe in children. Instead of simply saying our children have short attention spans, our philosophy is to make their attention spans longer. They can't cope in mainstream society otherwise. By its very nature, music helps ease the work of being disciplined. For many of these children, classical music is new and exciting. Most of the children do not come here with a fear of learning this music, widely considered to be the domain of the elite. They become more interested when they see me and our conductors perform and talk enthusiastically about the great works of Western civilization. It's not that these children can't appreciate the music; they have not been exposed to the works of the masters, composers such as Haydn, Schubert, and Bruckner, many of whom were boy choristers themselves. Enthusiam is infectious.

Our children gain a certain sophistication as a result of their learning about different languages, different countries, different types of people and cultures. As the boys get older and master the basic techniques, we spend time explaining the meanings of different works in order to further prepare them for performances. We talk about the work's orgin, composer, and message. Take *Zigeunerlieder*, opus 103, of Johannes Brahms. He wrote the music to capture expressions of love, compassion, and joie de vivre. The gypsies, who were largely hated and victimized throughout Europe, had an experience akin to the one of African-Americans in this country. The eleven songs making up opus 103 take on a deeper meaning as a result of our discussions. The music becomes their own because they understand not only the words but also the historical context.

Their education is underscored by a developing appreciation of the arts. Music is for the soul, nurturing the heart and challenging the brain. We have used it as a vehicle to provide children with a classical education, classical in the original sense of providing an education in what is truly important: developing the character. That is not to downplay our primary goal of becoming a world-class performing arts organization. Both work hand-in-hand here, one integral to the success of the other. Music has the ability to cut through race and class, stripping a child, regardless of environment, to a bare soul. It did for me. Through singing, I can express my sorrow, my love, any human emotion. It's easy because music is my soul. For many people, especially African-American children, singing is a little used way to educate. Singing is a natural teacher and motivator: it moves the heart and forces one to feel the range of human emotions. It's deeper than working out. It's an experience that can leave singers absolutely drained after performances. There's an art to singing, requiring a tremendous use of every part of the body.

I've always felt strongly about singing and wanted to share that with children. There might be one or two who will experience the same thing that I have over the years. Their entire lives may then be fulfilled just from having the experience of singing. Even in cases where singing does not become a vocation, lives can be turned around or enhanced. Everyone takes something different from music. If used in its proper way, music can transform unpolished diamonds. We instill in these kids the belief that they can be the best at any thing they choose. Music lifts every voice, not just of children who can sing and dance well but also of those who are not blessed with natural talent yet still have a dream of becoming somebody.

It's ironic that what we called home training down South has now taken on a different name in schools across America—character education. It has become a movement of increasing momentum, triggered largely by the belief that the nation is morally rudderless. The problem is acute in many African-American communities, where the staggering statistics of teenage pregnancies, black-on-black violence, and incarceration rates demonstrate all too clearly the need for children to know the meaning of words such as respect, honesty, integrity, discipline, hard work, and love, regardless of America's blatant and subtle forms of racism. We have taught these values at the Boys Choir of

Harlem since the day we began. We have taken the four-teenth-century concept of a boys choir, where boys received an education as well as musical training, to a twentieth-century situation in Harlem. We established an elementary school in 1986 and have been gradually adding grades until we will go all the way up to twelfth grade in 1996. Our philosophy has remained the same: we teach values by applying them to everything that we do. You can't simply tell children about values. You must show them.

Take honesty. It is a two-way street and means that we do not betray the students who have placed their growth and development in our hands. We are honest with them and expect them to be honest with us. If we see them doing something wrong or antisocial, we stop and talk with them about their behavior. It's more than telling them that they were doing something unacceptable. We tell them why their behavior was wrong and what the consequences would be if they continued with that behavior. We level with each of our students in a way that they can understand. We tell them how they are doing and what they need to do to improve. When a student is doing well, we applaud and provide direction for further success. We talk about the good and the bad.

The children listen for the most part. We are able to capture their attention because we have something that they want—fame. Everybody needs and wants glory, to be known and to have their name in lights. Recognition is important to all of us. I use that basic human need to train children to achieve stardom, if not onstage, then in other professions. Call it coercion or bribery or whatever—it works. Most of the children who come here are very talented, but not all have the best grades. We are more interested in their desire to do and be better. That desire is important in order for them to improve and go to the next level not only in singing but in their academics as well. We cannot save all children, but there is a commitment here to have an impact on their lives, to make them better people. That requires sticking with them, believing in them. The children recognize that we are tough only because we want them to succeed. Our tone and philosophy is about success, and therefore the children and the parents trust us. We don't take the easy way out by throwing our hands in the air and turning our backs, arguing that these children are incapable of learning. Parents bring their children here because, in many cases, they want us to save them. Seventy-five percent of the parents are single women who want strong male figures in their sons' lives.

Because we have their attention during rehearsals (and now at the academy), we talk about establishing goals then, even with our fourth graders. We talk about attending college, and we expect everyone to do so. Our expectations are reinforced when alumni return and talk about their college experiences. The children in the choir actually see people from their neighborhoods who have gone on to further their education. The alumni come back and explain why having the discipline learned at the choir enables them to write a term paper instead of playing cards or hanging out all night with friends.

Our rehearsals have evolved over the years and serve as a launching pad for discussions on values and how they relate to music. A teacher may ask his class, "What does it mean to be honest?" A talk on honesty may be triggered by a song, especially one written in a different language. We will often come across unfamiliar words, and just to check, I'll ask someone if they know what one of them means. I expect them to know the meaning of each and every word in each and every song. If they don't know the meaning of a word, I expect them to at least raise their hand and ask. I prefer that they take the initiative and look up the word in a dictionary. But this is where honesty and integrity come in: if someone doesn't know the meaning of a word, he shouldn't simply sit there and pretend he does. That sort of academic dishonesty only hurts kids in the end and causes the music of the choir to suffer as a result. Without knowing the meaning of the words, it is impossible to interpret the meaning of the songs. A song about joy requires a different emotion and energy than one about sorrow. The importance of having integrity and character becomes clear.

The development of character doesn't happen in one or two talks, or for that matter over a year. It happens over a course of development that makes a child believe that success is a function of discipline, integrity, and loyalty. It's all in the learning process, and it comes together to create a natural environment for children to achieve success. Character development doesn't stop in the classroom; it's in everything the kids do, from walking the hallways to respecting others when they ask questions. Dress is a simple thing but becomes a major issue when trying to establish a disciplined environment. Children must be reminded that schools are not a democracy where they can wear what they want and come and go as they please. Go to any other school and you will see everybody wearing caps backward and sideways, standing around the hallways with attitude. That sort of chaos is not tolerated here.

I understand children's need to be fashionably hip, but I want them to understand that they can't go out and get jobs wearing those types of fashions. They need to know the importance of not wearing baseball caps in certain situations in this society. We don't allow our students to wear any hats inside the building. We also require them to wear neckties. Part of success is knowing when to dress up and when to dress down. Personal grooming is also very important: whether or not they have haircuts, whether their shirts are cleaned and tucked inside their pants, and whether they have on a belt on or not. The modern-style imitation of inmates in prison is very popular on the streets but not here. We explain to the children where that look comes from, that it is a fringe subculture that represents failure of one sort or another. We are about success, not prison. The importance of dress is not to be underestimated. As an added message, I mention the fact that the corporations manufacturing the hip clothes are getting rich, and the African-American community receives little in return.

Fighting is not tolerated here. It represents a failure to solve conflicts without violence, which is arguably one of the principal reasons that black males are murdered on the streets in phenomenal numbers. Conflict resolution and learning how to deal with disappointment are key elements to socialization. If a child is undisciplined, he behaves by acting on his first impulse: the result is often a fight. This behavior is learned and usually comes from what children see in their homes and on the streets. Television and movies definitely add to their simplified notions of how to solve conflicts. We make a distinction here: we punish the fighting, not the person. In fact, some of our most loyal members were considered bullies in their schools.

Donald Robertson was the class bully at P.S. 154. As a fourth grader, he intimidated most of the other students. He could fight and fight well. No one could imagine Donald becoming a singer for the Boys Choir of Harlem. When he came to audition, however, he really impressed me with his enthusiasm and his desire to learn how to sing. His behavior suggested that many of his teachers had misunderstood him and that he had a broader cultural awareness than he was getting credit for. His life was more than the fighting he had revealed at school.

He came from the St. Nicholas projects, where crack and other drugs were brazenly sold on stairwells and benches. He lived with his grandmother, who also housed her crack-addicted son. His grandmother prohibited her daughter from seeing Donald, her son, because of her chronic drug and alcohol abuse. His mother was homeless at the time, and occasionally Donald would see her in the street, disheveled and high. It didn't seem to bother him at first. He believed that everyone in his neighborhood was all right, and his mother or his uncle were not detrimental to his life. That changed one night when his uncle came in late, high on crack, and set fire to the bed Donald and his older brother were sleeping on. Donald woke up and saw his uncle in their room. The smoke awakened his grandmother. She quickly smothered the fire with blankets and rushed the children to the hospital. She also asked police to issue a warrant for her son's arrest. Donald would later testify against his uncle in court.

The experience shook him up considerably. During our many talks, I told him that there would be many other experiences in his life that might change his attitude about people. But he had to understand that he had his own life to live and he could choose the path traveled by some of his relatives or not. From that day, Donald has been a fixture at the Boys Choir of Harlem. He attended the academy and spent at least ten hours a day at the BCH, including the time he simply hung around. He told me that one of the

The Turnbull men, standing outside the Manhattan School of Music, where I had just received my Doctorate of Musical Arts. (Left to right:) Sam Turnbull; Sam's sons Jason, whom I'm holding, Sam Jr, and Horace.

At a family gathering, I have my arm around my father's waist as we stand next to my sister Mary.

Two choristers receive pointers on fishing as they break from rehearsals during summer camp at the Kent School near the Housatonic River in Kent, Connecticut.

A rehearsal inside the Dempsey Multi-Service Center.

Aisha Favid, my first administrative assistant, preparing her son, Abdul-Malik, for performance.

Damon Kanes gave me this photograph as proof that he had made something of his life despite dropping out of the Boys Choir of Harlem.

A performance of **Amahl and the Night Visitors***, staged by Geoffrey Holder.*

Students raise their hand during class at the Choir Academy of Harlem.

Several choristers pose with Maurice Hines outside the City College of New York.

Betty Ford, Lady Bird Johnson, and Barbara Bush greet
choristers after a White House performance.

The choir with Ray Charles during the unveiling of "New Coke" at Radio Music Symphony Hall.

With my good friend Steven Sims.

A gathering of friends, staff, and boys during summer camp at Skidmore College.

Choristers "listen to the rain" during the "Spiritual Heritage" portion of our performances, much like Mahalia Jackson did during her rendition of "Didn't It Rain."

main reasons he stayed so much was that the BCH was the one place where good things were happening, where he didn't have to see, as he described them, "the bad things in the streets."

It takes courage to be a member of the choir. In this society, boys don't want to be in a choir largely because of the perception that choir members are soft or are sissies. A choir is not viewed as a team that requires physical and mental abilities but rather as something for girls or boys who could not cut it on the football field or the basketball court. By no means are these young men weak or afraid. On several occasions, some of our boys wrongly decided to fight to prove that they were tough. A lot of people forget that some of our boys come from the projects, too. A few of the fights have resulted in broken bones. We try to discourage them from getting into situations where they feel the need to resort to violence. The whole macho thing, especially among young black males, is pervasive and has little to do with toughness but everything to do with ego. We don't want our boys to run away from any challenge. But we encourage them to use their strength and courage to simply walk away, and let the taunts vanish into the air they leave behind.

Many of the children face a myriad of pressures, seemingly coming from every direction, creating a swirl of confusion: family problems, the pull of the streets, their own raging hormones. Having courage is easier said than done, and many are unable to muster the strength to persevere. José Cruz had such a challenge. He had a beautiful voice. He lived in a largely Hispanic neighborhood and had lots of older brothers who influenced his life tremendously. Their influence led to his leaving the choir. His brothers taunted him about singing. They thought he was too big physically to belong to a choir and that he should be playing baseball instead. The choir could balance the disparate forces in his life to a certain degree, but he needed a supportive family to help sort things out.

He lived in a crime-ridden neighborhood, on one of the heavier blocks for drug trafficking, 160th Street in Manhattan, between Amsterdam and Broadway. Frank Jones walked him home on several occasions at night because he was afraid to pass by all of the drug dealers alone. Because many of the drug dealers on his blocks were Hispanic, he developed a low opinion of his own people. He saw that people of color, at least in his neighborhood, were usually involved in crime. He did not understand all of the reasons for their behavior, but in his mind, he concluded that all people of color were bad, and conversly, that all white people were good. Quite naturally, then, he wanted to be around whites more than he did his own people.

He didn't really have anyone in his family whom he could turn to for advice. His father, who was almost Caucasian-looking, had moved out and lived around the corner with a younger woman. For a while, José could not accept the relationship. If he wanted to see his father, he had to deal with the presence of his father's girlfriend. José's view on relationships was clouded by his father, who could provide little help in sorting things out. The one brother who was somewhat sympathetic to José singing in the choir fell to the streets. The brother needed to support a woman who was having his baby. He spoke little English, was unemployed, and had to make some money.

José wanted to take on a new identity if he could, and he knew that he could if he was given the chance. Fortunately for him, his mother moved to a quieter neighborhood in Upper Harlem. José felt more comfortable there and was glad that he finally had escaped the neighborhood that made him feel less-than. He also wanted to leave the Boys Choir of Harlem. His mother was almost heartbroken. She was so proud of her son. She had seen him sing solos, some of which were featured on television. He told me that he wanted to see more Hispanics in the choir, but I knew it was much more than that. Based in part on our recommendation, José had been accepted to a Catholic school where there were hardly any Hispanics. He had an opportunity to go a Catholic school that was predominantly Hispanic, but he didn't want to do that and chose the predominantly white school instead. José didn't realize that his career at the Boys Choir could inspire other Hispanics to join. He needed to be a pioneer in that respect, but at the time, he just wasn't ready to accept that responsibility. We have stayed in touch with him, and there is talk that he might come back, which would be blessing for him and the choir.

The most critical element in providing character education is the parents. All too often, parents are allowing schools to teach their children values by default. They are so busy trying to earn a living—or in some cases doing drugs and alcohol—that they don't take the time to monitor or participate in the development of their children. Some are really too young to know how to raise their children, and as a result, their relationship with their kids is one of friendship, not of a parent or leader. Others are too busy or just don't care. The sad part is that most schools can't do it alone. When I taught junior high students in East Harlem, I saw a lot of children really interested in music. They wanted to work hard and were excited about learning. A success was seen every day, but at the same time it was very frustrating. The parents, unfortunately, were nowhere to be found. If I had stayed in the public school system, I guess I would be looking forward to retirement, walking around the hallways with little consciousness, much like a significant number of teachers do now. I definitely would not have had the courage to buck the system, which, by all accounts, is inflexible and unable to change to meet the needs of minority children. It seems that the system, thick with bureaucracy and political fiefdoms, is intended to stifle creativity and maintain the status quo, which means that parental involvement is minimal. Even when parents are involved, their political naïveté renders them powerless to effect positive change. Most are uneducated and uninformed and believe that the sixties strategy of screaming is all that is necessary. Those days are over. The reality is that a high percentage of minority children drop out or graduate unprepared to compete in a technologically advanced society. Some teachers argue that they can't teach their students for a variety of reasons, one of which is fear: fear that they might be beaten up or killed if they establish any sense of discipline in their classroom, fear that they might be sued by a disgruntled parent for abusing their child, physically or mentally. Teachers can't say too much to some children without receiving the wrath of a mother: "Don't you talk to my children like that; they have rights."

Rights? You earn your rights. The vicious cycle continues because these are the same kids, uneducated and ill prepared, who are out there on the streets, looking for a job, legal or illegal. People must survive and are willing to do anything to make a dollar. When children are not educated, society pays in the long run: more dysfunction, more crime, more prisons. Many of the children that come to the Boys Choir of Harlem are underprepared. We reestablish the basics about who they are and what we want to see accomplished. We do that through the type of music that's chosen, the variety of music, and the intensity and seriousness with which we pursue excellence. More than anything, belief is a prerequisite for their success. Many white and some black teachers do not believe these children are worth two cents and, as a result, have little respect for their intellectual capabilities. Such teachers do not expect anything from these students and fail to demand anything.

Many parents trust us: their actions confirm the African proverb that it takes a village to raise a child. Most choir parents are supportive and, more important, involved. We have parent meetings. The parents sponsor a concert every year. We encourage them to talk with counselors and teachers. The boys, especially those who are performing, know that we are connected with their parents. Mere mention of talking with their parents straightens out many of them without much of a fuss, but others are insolent at home and are unchecked by their parents or guardians. They remain so here. We face an unusual situation in that parents are often disappointed that their children are not selected to go on tour. We explain to them that we have high standards and that not all children blossom at the same time. In a sense, we are training parents as well. It's extraordinarily important that parents understand that they cannot be starry eyed and live vicariously through their children. They, too, must have the patience to allow their child to grow. No one can rush that. But as on any other team, choir children must earn their right to perform. Many parents don't quite know what to expect. We have generations of people who have grown up basically with a poverty mentality. These parents expect institutions to give them something for nothing, or worse, believe that we are public servants and therefore owe them something. We don't owe a thing to anyone here at the boys choir. It requires hours upon hours of work on a daily basis to achieve excellence, and there is no substitute.

The best way to involve the parents is through the children. When a child receives an opportunity to go on tour, he has an incentive to talk with his parents. The children know how to get everything from their parents, including $100 sneakers. I make it very clear: if you want to go to Japan, then I need you to improve your grades in a particular subject or I need you to straighten out a problem with a teacher or I need you to stop being a disruption during classes. There are students who are, for the most part, good: they're quiet, they do well in school, they have talent. More often than not, their success is the result of a certain kind of parent, one who is encouraging, sensitive, and fair. If a child doesn't have that at home, then I take it upon myself to become a surrogate parent.

Love is one of the key lessons at the Boys Choir of Harlem. Among the most difficult challenges I face is teaching children the true meaning of the word "love." It's tragic these days when children are more concerned with material things than with the love of their parents. They equate love with something somebody bought them, and it's just plain wrong. The children must understand what true love is about if they are to understand their parents' desire to protect them, to help develop their abilities. But as with every other value, you must show children how to love and explain love to them when appropriate situations arise. It's okay at the Boys Choir to say "I love you." It's okay to call each other brothers. It's okay to hug one another.

Charles Jackson typifies a child not understanding love. He came from a family of ten children, some of whom had gone on to college. They lived in the Lincoln projects, where his father, a storefront minister, was a superintendent for one of the high-rise buildings. The building was filled with working-class people, and as such, was considered to be the best in a complex mired in poverty and drugs. His parents were both born in Barbados and had a very disciplined, hardworking lifestyle. Charles was very talented, personable, and outgoing. He also had a very positive attitude until he became an adolescent. He had developed negative ways then, especially when he wanted to impress the girls or boys on the block. He tried to be a bully and was constantly involved in fights.

Charles had a terrible stammer, and he was small. He wanted others to consider him important and tough. He did everything to make other young men he considered tough comfortable around him. He wore the droopy pants below his butt, his hat backward, his sneakers untied. He attended a junior high school where there was a mixture of students: some had been held back, others had grown too old to stay in elementary school. Education was not taken seriously there. He got through largely because of his association with the Boys Choir of Harlem. He stood out in that environment. He was able to wave it as a flag. He knew he had a leg up on most of the other children. Charles was not ashamed of being in the BCH. He portrayed the choir as a cross between the Wild West and being a world traveling organization. He wanted them to think that the choir was rough and tough.

Charles had a good heart, but he always wanted to please

people on the street. He didn't want or seek the approval of studious types. His need to seek approval from friends outweighed seeking approval from authority figures. Because of that, he would repeat mistakes time and time again. He just didn't want to do right despite the benefits of a solid background. His family tried to raise him in the church. His mother and father were nice people and were good role models, but he remained rebellious and indifferent. I recall one of the major turning points in his life. His mother had been pregnant, but the baby died. The death saddened Charles. It made him stop and think about his life, how he was always taking things from other people. Someone finally had taken something from him. He became a little more humble. He had a sense of what it was like to lose something valuable.

But the experience did not stop his often belligerent behavior. We saw him hanging around corners with drug dealers. His fights at the choir continued to the point where we had to ask him to leave. We believe in punishing the crime, not the person, but Charles simply would not listen to or heed our advice. I remember him crying in my office when I told him that he could no longer be a member of the choir. He told me that he really wanted to stay if we would give him yet another chance. And then he said something that sticks with me. "My parents don't love me," he cried. It just came out. He was desperate at the time, but there was probably something deeper that he felt yet could not explain.

The truth of the matter was that his parents loved him very much and wanted the very best for him. There was no doubt about their love for him. They bailed him out of many situations. But Charles did not see what love was really about. Love is not giving your kid permission to stay out until two in the morning, as so many of them do. Charles's parents were strict and stern; they were very protective. He misinterpreted that and felt that his parents should be loose and free and unconcerned, like many of the parents of his friends. Charles would later be convicted for his role in a murder. He denied any involvement and claimed that others did the actual deed. He received a four-to-eight-year sentence.

The ability to love is a function of self-esteem, which is at the heart of transforming young men. The boys feel good about themselves when they are onstage and associated with the Boys Choir of Harlem. Glory touches them and affects them in a profound, everlasting way. Even if they make mistakes later in their lives, the children know for at least several nights that they are the center of attention, performing in an internationally renowned group. Their self-esteem is further bolstered when we help them learn how to make the right choices in life and strengthen their courage to do the right thing. We talk with the boys constantly. Sometimes those discussions involve their academics. Other times, it's their development as musicians and singers. It's not how the students come to the choir; it's how they are when they leave. Self-esteem is a function of hard, hard work. Children who think little of themselves are usually negative, afraid to try, and very reluctant to open up. When we are teaching a new song, for instance, a child with low self-esteem won't even try to learn, or worse, won't care if he learns or not. That sort of behavior is a red flag. Some never improve, but the majority can with counseling and tutoring. Once a child feels respected, once he understands how important it is to be honest, once he knows what it means to be loyal, he will act differently, and usually for the better. Children automatically develop self-esteem because they have a better sense of who they are and what their purpose is. All of that is essential to the basic philosophy of the BCH: to take children to a higher level.

For one thing, these characteristics send the right message and give potential detractors less to say or write about. As our reputation as a first-class musical organization grew around the world in the early eighties, critics began looking for every little crack. We had too much to lose, too much at stake, and too many serious problems to remedy. For the most part, we received favorable media coverage. "The real surprise of the afternoon was the ability of the Boys Choir of Harlem to cope with the stylistic and technical difficulties of Bach's music. Harlem Goes Bach gave much pleasure to a large and enthusiastic audience," Raoul Abdul wrote in the *Amsterdam News* in 1981. "This choir, expertly guided by director Walter J. Turnbull, is one of the finest groups of its kind, splendidly disciplined in tone quality, precision, balance, and intonation," Bill Zakariasen wrote in the *New York Daily News* in 1983. "The highlight of the Boys Choir of Harlem's Sunday evening all-Mozart recital was a sinuous and propulsive presentation of the *Requiem* (K. 626). . . . The choir sang with winning enthusiasm," wrote Tim Page of *The New York Times* in 1983.

Another *New York Times* reviewer caught a different side of the choir. Theodore H. Libbey, Jr., was sitting offstage in the back of the Church of the Intercession when we were performing *Amahl and the Night Visitors*, which Geoffrey Holder staged and costumed for the production in 1982. As the choir lined up to make their entrance, a boy named Gordon Logan had a problem with another choir member. A scuffle ensued: nothing serious, just enough of a commotion to draw the attention of the reviewer. Our performance was wonderful, and the reviewer acknowledged that in part. But Libbey also threw in a zinger: "Pitch was a significant problem for the boys choir, which showed good energy in its singing but needs more discipline."

More discipline. The words struck a sensitive nerve. If the reviewer only knew the struggle we faced collectively, as an organization, and individually, as in the case of Gordon Logan. The writer's criticisms might have been aimed only at our music, but for some reason, I could not help but think the scuffle had colored his observations. If only the writer knew Gordon and his brother Eric, and the value we place on discipline. It is probably the major tenet of our philosophy. I define discipline as establishing a goal and having the ability to overcome obstacles to accomplish that goal. It has to do with a person's ability to focus. Most people think of discipline as simply a matter of punishment. That is not discipline in its entirety but rather one of the central links of the chain of character. As with most values, discipline is not learned in a day or a week; it is learned over the course of years and requires constant reinforcement, not only by teachers but by parents as well. Both Gordon and his brother Eric had problems beyond our abilities to solve. We only had the three or four hours a day of rehearsal time to give them; they needed much more.

They came to us from P.S. 28. Eric was the older. Their mother was young, single, and had a very bad drinking problem. Their neighborhood on 150th and Broadway was a major drug haven, and they stayed inside their apartment much of the day and night. They were not permitted to venture too far outside because of all the shoot-outs. Their mother basically needed somewhere for them to go during the day. Gordon was very quiet at first, and all of a sudden, he became rowdy. He was not a quick learner and, in fact, could not even read at the age of ten. His teachers rarely paid him any attention. His singing was all right. The brothers were considered to be sheltered kids in a sense. Their behavior and personalities suggested otherwise, especially Eric's. He teased and made fun of other people; he put others down to build himself up. Their problems became worse when they began attending junior high school. Eric was really just being mischievous, and that became part of his identity. We were always calling his mother in to the office for conferences triggered by something Eric had done. He was always trying to show off. The mother's response was simple: "Well, I want y'all to do something with them." It was not so much that she didn't have control. She believed that giving them material things was enough. If they didn't appreciate the material things, then they just didn't appreciate her as a mother. She didn't realize that she had to get in the trenches and fight every battle, incident by incident, in order to make those children respect her. She wasn't willing to do that.

The sad part about both these young men is that Eric ended up dropping out of high school. He eventually joined the army but would later receive a dishonorable discharge for insubordination and possession of drugs. His mother came in afterward and tried to persuade me to write recommendation letters to potential employers for Eric. She told me that she was sorry that he had dropped out of the choir and wished that he had stayed. We never wrote any letters on his behalf because he never showed us his discharge papers. The next thing I knew, Eric was supposedly attending Fairleigh Dickinson University on a basketball scholarship. That turned out to be a lie. He was later busted for possession of crack and did a four-year prison sentence.

His brother fared worse. Gordon went on a violent streak; he stabbed a student at public school. The family of the youngster pressed charges against Gordon, and his mother kicked him out of her apartment. He went to live at a group home and within a few weeks stabbed another youngster. Gordon was sociopathic and was sent to prison, where he was involved in another fight. But this time, the other inmate stabbed him with a shank; he died in prison.

It's very easy to simply say these children need more discipline. The reality of instilling self-discipline is much more complicated, the task Sisyphean. Sometimes it is too late for some of these children; they've made decisions in their lives that resulted in drug addiction or prison. But in most cases it isn't too late. Though some of the children have made mistakes, they know in their hearts how to separate right from wrong and how to go forward. That includes some of the children who were asked to leave the choir for behavorial problems. It's ironic, then, that another *New York Times* writer, Will Crutchfield, had a completely different perspective when he wrote a review on June 13, 1985:

The Boys Choir of Harlem is a testament to discipline, high standards, and commitment. Take for example, its pronunciation of German, as one could at the choir's 10th anniversary concert at the Alice Tully Hall. Ordinarily the idea of a choir singing in a language foreign to its members and audience is questionable—and it is usually done badly. But here, in Bach's *Christ lag in Todesbandem*, the subtlest distinctions—the specific quality of the closed vowels, for example—had been aimed for and usually achieved. The thought of these young people joyously embracing the sort of challenge that achievement represents is nothing less than a clarion call to optimism.

Roger Holland wanted to sing. The seed was planted in late 1980 when he became a member of the choir at Our Lady of Charity Church in Bedford-Stuyvesant and grew when he watched the ABC special *From Harlem to Haarlem*. He had been watching television and noticed a group of black boys singing classical music. He thought it unusual at first. Like most, he saw blacks singing only pop or jazz or gospel. But not classical, and definitely not in Europe by a group from Harlem. He was impressed. He had been studying classical music as a pianist at the New York School of Performing Arts and had received private lessons as well. He was not unfamiliar with the works of the masters, but classical choral music was new—and exciting. His only problem was figuring out a way to become a member.

He found the answer in church. Donna Brown was an assistant conductor at the Boys Choir of Harlem and had just started working at his church as an organist and choir conductor. She mentioned to him that the Boys Choir needed tenors and basses. The audition was on a holiday, Presidents' Day. Holland was early. Dressed in a sweater and neatly pressed slacks, he came to the Church of the Intercession and waited for the audition to start. There may have been about sixty kids in the choir at that time, and many of them were watching a movie about the Vienna Boys Choir in the church's common room. From that day on, Holland has been a part of the Boys Choir of Harlem. His career has spanned a period of phenomenal growth, and he is one of our success stories. As a pianist, he has exceptional skills in pop, jazz, gospel, and classical, a rare combination, and even rarer among African-Americans.

More important, Holland had integrity from the start. He knew not to talk back to an adult or leave his house looking a mess with disheveled clothes and uncombed hair. He always wanted to do and be right, paying attention to details and doing what he was told. He was always on time, very serious about his music, and eager to learn more. His parents instilled in him a sense of values through their own example. His father worked as an English teacher at a junior high school in Coney Island. His mother held a variety of jobs throughout her life and worked as the executive assistant for the director of Black Ministries, a black Catholic organization. "I knew what it was like to be yelled at for doing something wrong," he told me later. "My mother wasn't going to raise a fool for a son."

Roger wanted to learn choral music. I remember his audition at the Church of the Intercession. Right before he began singing, he leaned over and told me that he didn't think that he was a tenor. He was a junior at the New York School of Performing Arts and had read some books describing the range of the tenor voice, which he thought he couldn't match. He had just turned sixteen and his voice had begun to settle. "My range is not very wide, and once I get past G, I have trouble singing up there," he explained. "I think I'm a baritone." I was struck by his honesty and his knowledge of his voice. I told him not to worry. "Being able to sing high notes doesn't necessarily make you a tenor," I said. "It really depends on the color and timbre of your voice." I knew he didn't quite understand, but he sang "Lately," a Stevie Wonder song, and played the piano. His vocal abilities definitely could be honed, and he was truly a fine musician. We selected him in 1981 as much for his skills as for his character. He was very happy. "For me it was being a part of something musical," he told me recently. "Because of my own love of singing and choir, I just ate everything up. Whatever I could get. It was like a love affair. Just to be able to be there was very special."

Roger was an exception: his family life was stable and solidly middle class. They lived in the Flatbush section of Brooklyn, near East New York. Their block was neat, their tidy three-story row house standing as an exception to the trash-strewn, broken-down neighborhoods that plague portions of Brooklyn and, for that matter, much of Harlem. Roger was talented, but no more talented than scores of other children that we have seen over the years. The difference was that Roger's mind was free to pursue his goals. His parents had the wherewithal to afford piano lessons, and they had the fortitude to raise him in a strong church community—an even more invaluable lesson. Roger was fortunate. My job was to give that opportunity to others less fortunate.

Rehearsals back in the early 1980s for tenors and basses were usually held twice a week at the Church of the Intercession. Altos and tenors rehearsed at least four times a week. Holland was a junior when he began. After school, he would catch a subway uptown. At the end of his day, he would ride about ninety minutes on the train to go back home. Performances were usually on weekends in order not to interfere with school schedules, and there were not nearly as many as there would be later.

For many of the children, rehearsals were much different from their classes. In those settings, teachers presented certain concepts, facts, and figures and expected the children to learn them. There was little classroom discussion or participation by students. For the most part, they sat there numb, trying to absorb as much information as they could in order to spew it back out for exams. I taught music during rehearsals, which by definition required student participation and involvement.

The music generates camaraderie. The children work together to achieve a certain goal, much like any other team. They cooperate with one another, help one another, support one another, and listen to one another. They blend their voices together, come in on the downbeat together, and breathe together. I constantly remind the boys that the team is only as strong as its weakest link. After a while, they develop a bond based on their music. During the mid-eighties, many of the boys lived in Central Harlem or were members of Ephesus Church. Because Holland lived in Brooklyn, he didn't have much in common with most of the other boys outside of choir. He was introverted, not very socially outgoing. He saw his involvement with the choir as business. At the end of rehearsal, he went home, rarely hanging around with the other boys. Nonetheless, differences over geography eventually faded away, and Roger Holland developed strong friendships in the choir that have lasted more than a decade.

The intangibles are important. I make selections for tours based first and foremost on whether the children know their music. But if children don't attend rehearsals or are rude and disrespectful, they can't go. Of roughly sixty children we had in the performing choir at the time, we usually selected about twenty. Holland was in the performance choir right from the start and stayed on after he graduated from high school. He spent a year at Brooklyn College and then transferred to Westminster Choir College in Princeton, New Jersey, specializing in music and choir. He received a bachelor's degree from Westminster and later received a master's degree in piano performance from the Manhattan School of Music in 1992.

Holland became the choir's accompanist after high school. He played pop music during rehearsals, and when we lost Donna Brown, he stepped in and filled her position. He was much younger and less experienced than his predecessors, but I believed in him. Of course, he was scared to death the first time he played during a performance. To eliminate his anxiety, I worked him hard during rehearsals. I knew how he hated to be yelled at and used that to my advantage. "He was on me all the time," Holland remembers. "He would say things like, 'No, that's not right, that's not the chord.' A lot of times, even if I was right and the band was wrong, he would yell at me."

Holland performed well and would later become a teacher at the boys choir, which by the mid-eighties was experiencing a number of successes but still remained a struggling, nonprofit performing arts organization. The burden on my staff was incredible: not only did we demand musical excellence, we also had to save the lives of children. I developed a two-pronged attack. I applied to the New York public school system in the early 1980s to open an elementary school, grades four through six, and I stepped up fund-raising efforts. Those efforts were long-range and mired in bureaucracy and, in the case of our board of directors, incompetence. Even though the choir had achieved a modicum of success, fund-raising was difficult because everyone thought that our organization had ample resources. They looked at our spiffy performances, heard about our international and national tours, and wrongly concluded that we were awash in dough. Nothing could be further from the truth. The lack of money was also the result of the unwillingness of the majority of our board members to pound on the doors of corporations and foundations. Many of them were satisfied with simply being associated with a world-class performance group and had no idea of the work involved in getting the boys ready for concerts. That is not to say that all our board members were unproductive or unsupportive. Jane Boyer and Steve Simms, to name two, were unflinching in their dedication.

Even good news sometimes turned out bad. In 1982 we received a $250,000 challenge grant from the National Endowment for the Arts. In order to receive the federal funds, we needed to raise three times that amount from private sources. The money would have enabled the Boys Choir of Harlem to have a cash reserve that we could borrow from for artistic development. It would also enable the organization to stabilize its finances and become a more solid institution. "We have lived hand-to-mouth," I told the *New York Daily News*. "The staff has sometimes gone without a paycheck. The choir exists because many people have made sacrifices." I explained to the newspaper that my goal was to get everyone in Harlem to donate a single dollar "or more if they have it. This is the chance for people to put their money where their hearts are. People are always telling me how proud they are of the boys. Well, now they can do a little more." I didn't tell anyone that I had to work a job under the Comprehensive Education and Training Act (CETA) and drive a cab to make ends meet. If it wasn't for my brother Horace and his wife leaving groceries in my refrigerator, I don't know how I would have made it through those early days. They also gave me a car. It was an old lime green Chevy Nova, and the boys used to laugh at the age, the color, and the fact that I had to prop up the front seat with a two-by-four. I had holes in my shoes, which, of course, the boys noticed. Most of my energy went to the choir. We had traveled to Italy, Austria, Germany, and Finland to perform in major festivals. But we couldn't raise enough money at home to qualify for the NEA grant.

The board was unable to get the job done. They established a fund-raising committee, which also did little. Part of the reason was that Franklin Williams had promised to head up the committee before the NEA awarded the grant. When we received the grant, Williams backed out, leaving the choir high and dry for the second time. I remember when I had to call officials at the NEA and ask them to reduce the amount of our grant to $150,000. It still hurts. But there was no way we were going to raise $750,000. No way.

The lack of resources could be seen in the fatigue of our staff. For instance, an organization would hire us to perform a big event, promising good money. But it would mean that the boys would have to learn music in a very short period of time, which required a lot of conductors to break the music into sectionals. If we could hire four or five teachers, then the learning could be that much quicker. Sometimes, we could stretch the budget to make the hires. Other times, the staff had to stretch themselves to the limit. There was never any time to resolve these issues. Things were moving fast. Demands for performances were coming more frequently, and we needed to earn all the money that we could to help pay for tutors, counselors, and music teachers. My more immediate concern, however, was maintaining the balance between our high musical standards and our vital social services. We tried to hire teachers who were not only extremely talented but also sensitive to the needs of the children. Without the music, we had little; without well-adjusted boys, we had even less.

I looked for several skills in hiring staff. The most important was outstanding musicianship. We had an excellent choir and could not afford a mediocre teacher who could not help us attain higher levels of performance. That standard alone created a problem: New York City was filled with excellent musicians, only a few of whom wanted to come to Harlem and teach children. I wanted some kind of teaching experience in their backgrounds or some sort of commitment to help children make something out of their lives. That combination was extraordinary. We needed continuity: the children needed to have adults in their lives on a consistent basis. My task, then, was daunting. For every ten applicants, maybe one fit the bill.

One of them was Steve Pane. He grew up in Northport, Long Island and earned a bachelor's degree from the Manhattan School of Music, my alma mater, and a master's degree from Westminster Choir College in Princeton, New Jersey. He started part-time as a conductor and pianist at the end of 1985 and went full-time in 1986. We had brought him in because we needed extra assistance to help the boys quickly learn Andrew Lloyd Webber's *Requiem* in time for a performance. He came at an exciting time. President Ronald Reagan honored us with the 1986 Presidential Volunteer Action Award in 1986. We left the Church of the Intercession after ten great years. Our organization had grown from twenty boys and an annual budget of about $20,000 to about two hundred children and a 1986 budget of about $1 million. We moved to the Dempsey Multi-Service Center on Lenox Avenue and struck a lease agreement with the city of New York. Although we had begun talking with city officials about the Dempsey Center several years earlier, bureaucracy coupled with construction delays forced us to wait. The building was less than promised. It was a dilapidated former school building that had been renovated to a degree, but the workmanship was shoddy.

Steel grates and sheets of plastic covered the broken windows. The unfinished floors buckled in hundreds of places. Radiators made a lot of noise but gave off little heat.

Undeterred, we opened the Boys Choir of Harlem Academy there. The elementary school was part of a partnership with New York Community School District No. 5 and provided a complete education. The teachers were employees of the school district and provided lessons in math, reading comprehension, science, history, writing, and spelling consistent with the state's curriculum. The academic program comprised three elements: the regular classroom sessions; an enrichment program, which afforded the children an opportunity to talk with practitioners in various professions and go on field trips; and the tutorial program, which offered extra help after school and before choir rehearsal. The academy was special. We had a computer lab. Citibank and Digital had outfitted the entire organization and provided donations and technical know-how. We also had a piano lab, where we gave children free lessons and improved the abilities of others more experienced. Our academic programming, with its heavy concentration in music, was rare in New York City. Funding for most after-school programs never recovered after the city's 1975 fiscal crisis. Of the forty-one hundred teachers who lost their jobs during that budget crunch, more than 40 percent of them were instructors in the visual arts, music, and physical education, according to a private report.

Steve Pane's main responsibilities were first as a conductor, then as an administrator. He ran the arts department for the newly created school. He really didn't know that much about counseling. Most of what he learned over the years came from Frank Jones, who taught him how and how not to talk to children: how to establish respect and friendship while maintaining a balance between the two.

Pane was lost when he first began teaching here. He had taken several education courses in the past but had little idea how to establish control in a classroom. He knew even less about establishing discipline. The kids just acted up in his room, so much so that he would order them to sing just to keep them quiet. After a while, he came to me for help. I understood his problem. I was the same way when I first started teaching in the public schools until an old veteran, Asta Hairston, whose cousin Jester was a composer and television star on the series *Amen*, sat me down and shared her years of experience. I invited her to sit in on Pane's classes. Her diagnosis was quick and sure: "Honey, you don't have any presence."

Asta had gotten right to the heart of one of the most fundamental problems in education—the teachers. It is not so much what the teacher does in the classroom; it is where the teacher's head is. The children are very much attuned to sincerity and phoniness. More than anything else, that is what is so terrifying to teachers. Even the teachers who wanted to do well were too worried about whether the children liked them or not to really impart knowledge. Pane, like so many other teachers, wanted the children to respond to him as a person instead of gaining their respect as a teacher. Pane was forced to reevaluate his own needs and told me later that he grew more then than at any other time in his life. He really had to examine such fundamental questions as who he was, why he was at the choir, and did he really care enough about these kids to be and do what they needed. Further undermining his ability to teach was the issue of race. Pane, who is white, felt guilty and wanted these mostly black children to accept him as a white man. He grew up in a liberal household, one where everyone knew that racism was an evil thing and that the Ku Klux Klan was full of bad people. But the subtle racism, the negative preconceptions that even he had, were not exposed until he began actually teaching young black men. The questions about intelligence and character went right out the window when he started knowing some of the children. He learned about racism from the inside.

Some of the teachers came here and could not accept the fact that they couldn't reach these children. They rarely talked with me. But they would share their thoughts with Pane about the problem with what they would call "animals" and worse. Pane became enraged at such conversations and would launch into a diatribe about how the teachers were failing the children, not the other way around. Pane told them that it was fairly simple to establish order and respect in a classroom. The first thing is to assign seats and have class time organized in such a way that the children know that the first ten minutes will be exercises, the next fifteen lecture, and so on. Every day, then, the children know what to expect. Once the discipline has been established, the children can begin learning. There is such a negative connotation to discipline; it almost implies that a teacher is beating a child. No: it's about establishing a structure and expectations in a way that children can understand. Pane was also respectful and civil. He always began his classes, "Good morning, gentlemen."

It's one thing to read about an act of racism in the newspaper but completely different to see it with your own eyes. Pane remembers countless children that he worked with over the years. He would watch them stand with a shirt and tie on in the streets of Harlem, waiting to catch a cab, only to have them tell him that it would be better if they stood on the sidewalk and let him hail the cab. Sure enough, the cab would stop. Fortunately for the choir, Pane resolved those issues and by his second year put everything together. He understood what we were trying to do at the Boys Choir of Harlem and became one of our finest teachers. He taught the teachers as well as the children. He discovered that some teachers were neither willing to learn nor willing to change their old ways. Those teachers didn't understand the depth of the organization. There is no other boys choir in the world with our combination of performance, academics, and counseling. Pane got it, and was able to teach music and values at the same time. He accepted tasks with children facing tremendous challenges and never complained. His only question was how he could do more.

Yuseff Washington was one of the children to whom Steve gave his all to help. Yuseff had been taken from his crack-addicted mother, and moved to a foster home and then to his grandmother's. Later, when he reentered the foster-care system, he was assigned to a home in Queens, which meant that he couldn't get to the boys choir, the one stable thing in his life. Steve worked the phones around the clock to find families near Harlem where Yuseff could live. He wrote letters, made phone calls, and probably would have let Yuseff live with him if he had the space in his one-bedroom apartment. More than anything, though, he spent time with Yuseff, listening to him, helping him get through his struggle without losing his mind.

Back in 1986, Yuseff had come to his first rehearsal at the Boys Choir of Harlem with his grandmother. She was very kind and soft-spoken. But it was obvious that she had an unusual lifestyle. She dressed in clothes that seemed like a costume. Her glazed eyes and scent of alcohol suggested she was no stranger to drinking. She loved Yuseff and wanted to do all that she could to make him a success. She had seen the choir on televison and read about us in the newspapers. She thought the choir would be a perfect match for her grandson. She had been a showgirl, a dancer, during the Harlem Renaissance. She believed that her daughter's son had inherited her singing and dancing talents. Drug and alcohol addiction had gotten the better of her daughter, who had been living in a welfare hotel in Manhattan. Yuseff lived with her for a while until he moved in with his grandmother a few months before he became a member of the choir. I remember him telling us about his living situation. Everything was done in one room. He kept his clothes there. He slept there. He ate there. When he was through with his dishes, he took them to the bathroom and washed them in the bathtub. He was so accustomed to washing dishes in the bathroom that when he moved in with his grandmother he did the same thing, even though she had a separate kitchen, bathroom, living room, and bedrooms.

Yuseff immediately adjusted to his grandmother's apartment. His sister, who is about four years older, moved in as well. She was incorrigible, staying out late at night, rarely showing up for school. His grandmother received no assistance for taking care of her daughter's children and eventually fell on hard times. Yuseff began to lose weight and show other signs of malnutrition. At that point, we decided to step in and save this child. Because of our efforts to help his grandmother, Yuseff began to forge an unbreakable relationship with the choir. He had seen everything the streets of New York had to offer: drug dealing, teenage prostitution, shootings, robberies. He knew where his future was headed and placed his devotion with the choir, which became his new family. Amazingly, he has a twinkle in his eye and is very much interested in learning. He has always wanted to do things that require discipline, things like coming to rehearsals, taking piano lessons. He has not become bitter or disenchanted with life and eagerly looks forward to the day when he can go to college.

"The Boys Choir of Harlem helped me out a lot," Yuseff told me recently. "To be honest, I don't know what I would be doing if I wasn't here. I'd probably be in jail or something. I really would." Coming from any other child, the statement could be readily dismissed as youthful bluster. But Yuseff grew up hard, virtually by himself, vulnerable to the streets and left alone to make decisions. His life caught the attention of state officials as a result of his grandmother's whimsical love. She had helped her daughter gain an apartment in Harlem. Yuseff, his two brothers, and his sister lived there with his mother. They got by on whatever money their mother earned. Most of the time, there was little food in the refrigerator. As Yuseff recalls, their mother stayed in the bathroom, high or passed out. One day his grandmother called to check on things; Yuseff told her everything was all right. Not convinced, she called the school and learned that Yuseff had missed fifty-five days. He was in the third grade at the time and skipped a lot because he was in charge of watching his four-year-old brother.

Social workers came to their house in a few days, only to discover the children in the house alone, the mother nowhere to be found. The oldest brother had moved out and lived on his own. The city placed Yuseff and his sister in a home in Queens; their younger brother went to a home in Staten Island. To keep the family somewhat intact, the city scheduled for the two middle siblings to visit the youngest. The family there immediately asked why the little boy didn't speak. He could talk, but he never said a word, only shaking his head whenever he wanted something or the mood struck him. That situation lasted for a few months before Yuseff's grandmother gained custody of the three youngest children in the fall of 1986, about the time he auditioned for the Boys Choir of Harlem.

Yuseff liked singing. He and his sister, who belonged to a church choir at the time, sang along with their radio whenever songs by Michael Jackson or Billy Joel came on. They made up little dance routines, and for that moment, they were big-time stars, unfazed by their depressing reality. When he went back to school, Yuseff auditioned for his school's choir. They promptly rejected him. He had also come here, and when his school discovered that he had become a member of Boys Choir of Harlem, they changed their minds and made him a member of their choir, too. Life was getting better for Yuseff. He was living with his grandmother, who busied herself with teaching him how to survive. She taught him how to cook, how to take out frozen meat in the morning so that at dinnertime it would be thawed and ready to cook. Yuseff was also making connections to his father's family. Even though his father had died by then, Yuseff felt a connection by talking with his father's brother, who had become a superintendent of an apartment building in Harlem. He would go over there and hang out for a while, listening to the stories about his father. He also learned about his cousins and several nieces and nephews.

The good times lasted for only a while. His sister and younger brother were too much for his aging grandmother. His sister eventually moved out and lived with her godfather. The youngest brother didn't really do anything bad; he went to school every day and was a pretty decent kid. But he wanted to have friends, and he liked to play video games. As Yuseff tells the story, he just didn't know when to come back home. He was about eight years old, hanging out until about 3 A.M. One night, the police brought him home. He had gone to a movie theater and posed as some man's child. He got in free, but the police saw him outside, late at night, alone. They picked him up; he gave them his address. They told his grandmother that she needed to keep a better eye on him, and that was it. Within days, social workers came to his brother's school and placed him in another foster home, this time in Brooklyn. A few days later, the choir held its Christmas party. We gave each of the boys portable tape players. When Yuseff came home, he found his little brother sitting in the living room, talking with their grandmother. He said that he had taken the subway. They went to sleep, dreaming about Christmas, and when they awakened police were at their door. They took his little brother back to his foster home and took Yuseff to a shelter until they found him a home. They eventually put the two boys together, thus continuing their odyssey from one foster home to another.

Steve Pane found out what was happening to Yuseff and immediately visited him at the shelter. Pane and Yuseff had become really close. In fact, many of the boys called Pane Yuseff's daddy and teased him relentlessly. Pane helped him a lot simply by being there for him. "It's a good thing I was with the boys choir," Yuseff told me. "I was moving around a lot those days and always knowing that the choir was there, it was kind of like an anchor. Different people I was with, it took them a little getting used to, like me, going out and then coming home at three in the morning or sometimes having to leave at four in the morning to catch a plane at six A.M." Pane understood the demands. "Whenever I had a problem, Mr. Pane was always there to talk to me, always there to help me with anything, especially with my schoolwork. I was doing horribly in math. He would stay late and tutored me. He gave me private piano lessons, a whole bunch of stuff."

Some of the neighborhood kids had seen Yuseff on television or in the newspaper. They provided support of sorts by asking him different questions about traveling and being in the choir. He had a little status. Young girls frequently asked him to sing for them. There was some jealousy among the young men, but for the most part, Yuseff was pretty humble about his celebrity. He made a practice of going to the neighborhood basketball court and shooting hoops as a way to get to know people. But our travel schedule is pretty demanding during the year, and he doesn't really have that much time to hang out.

More than anything else, Yuseff knows about hard work and discipline. "Sometimes it's difficult," he told me. "Say you want to do something but you know it's not the right thing but it's the most fun thing to do. You've got to kinda fight that off and do the right thing. Say, for instance, you really don't want to go to rehearsal, but you want to go play basketball or go to one of those video game arcades or something, but you know you have rehearsals and you have to get ready and know your music in order to get selected. So you have to kind of stick to it and go to rehearsal instead of doing what you want. Because after all, once you get selected to go somewhere, then you never know: you can always have time to do what you want because you might stop at a mall or something. You can go shopping or anything. Or say we finish all our homework and we have some free time. One time, I don't remember where we were but everyone finished their work and we had nothing to do. Dr. Turnbull took the whole choir to see *Dances with Wolves.*"

The
Struggle

THE BOYS FACED an uphill challenge. If they decided to pursue a career in music, they would compete against children whose parents who could afford to give them $50-per-hour piano lessons or send them to Juilliard Prep. Those kids had a tremendous head start. They began in the fourth grade and had ample resources. In order to compete, the boys needed to start their training just as early as the wealthier kids.

Gone were the days when a high school student could make up the difference with simple hard work. I remember my junior year in high school, when Mama and I drove Nannie's Chevy up the highway to a store near the outskirts of Greenville. She knew the troubles I had encountered at my friend Marianne's house trying to play her piano, and she wanted me to have my own. We went to the store and she bought a $700 spinet on layaway. She put $70 down, and they delivered it the next week. I played it day and night. In today's world, not that many poor families can make that kind of investment. Not many can afford piano lessons when they barely have enough money to feed and house themselves. For most of those interested in music, one of the few ways to gain experience was by joining a church choir or the school glee club. Those were fine as a start but did not have the wherewithal to prepare children to compete on the highest levels. Our curriculum then was designed to close that gap by giving the children who demonstrated an aptitude the same opportunity. We had pianos, classically trained musicians as teachers, and more important, time.

Steve Pane became director of the music school at the choir academy in 1989. He supervised the afternoon classes in voice, dance, and piano. These classes were held before rehearsals and were intended to further develop the children's individual abilities. Developing a curriculum proved difficult. For one thing, no textbooks existed for nine-year-olds singing Stravinsky. The books that were written were geared toward college-level students on the one hand and first graders on the other. We had to design our own curriculum, which is still evolving. We started with a basic question: how do we improve? Because of the uniqueness of the choir, we had a lot of possibilities. We had children that came here when they were nine years old, and many of them stayed until they were at least eighteen. They had the potential to leave the choir with a really thorough understanding of music.

The curriculum worked. We still performed difficult music in the mid-eighties, but our overall musicianship increased dramatically as a result of the academy. Before then, most of our students could not read music and were learning as best they could. There were a few who caught on, but they were unable to have the same impact as the entire performing choir attending music classes. You could hear the difference in the forcefulness of the sound. The choir had gained more confidence, executing the intricate double fugue in the third movement of Haydn's *Te Deum*, for instance, with better precision and more accuracy.

Our hard work and talent created more demand for performances. We went from doing thirty or forty shows a year in and around New York City to about one hundred shows in 1987, including a national and international tour. In December of that year alone, we did twenty shows in three different cities, including one week when we performed at seven different Christmas events. Our staging also became more dramatic. Instead of having the children stand in a semicircle, gathered around a piano dressed in their red gowns and white ruffled collars, they were now able to move about the stage in carefully choreographed steps. Our performances did not go unnoticed. Two months after our busy Christmas schedule, we headed to France to perform at the prestigious International Boys Choir Festival in Nantes. We were the only American group asked to do so that year. U.S. Representative Charles Rangel, Democrat from New York, called the choir "one of Harlem's finest exports. For the past twenty years, the choir has been proving to the world that Harlem is not a place of drugs, decay, and despair but of hope, joy, and achievement."

Performances were not the only thing in greater demand. By the late eighties, we held auditions for about 3,000 children a year when we were only able to admit about 90. Of the 150 kids enrolled in the academy and choir, only about 30 made the performing choir. The HBC had quickly become one of the organizations most sought after by parents throughout the city. The reason was quite simple: in a city where 72 percent of minority teenagers don't graduate from high school, 98 percent of choirboys go on to college. Barbara Bush recognized our achievements, and after our White House performance in June 1989, she told the gathering that "what the Boys Choir of Harlem represents is so important and optimistic that I wish that it could be replicated in every city and town in America." The choir had moved people to act from the heart. After a concert at New York's Waldorf-Astoria Hotel, the *Wall Street Journal* reported, the president of Virginia Union University in Richmond sought out soloist Gilbert Robinson and offered him a scholarship on the spot.

Morley Safer of *60 Minutes* asked an interesting question for his report on the Boys Choir of Harlem shown in December 1989: "What makes your kids different from the other kids that we read about, the ones that go out and assault people and use drugs?" My answer was clear. "My kids are no different," I told him. "They come from the same projects. They come from the same kinds of families. The difference is that there is somebody here willing to do something for them, and they are willing to do something. There is an opportunity here. The difference, then, is the opportunity."

My answer was based on what I had seen, read, and experienced over the years. Children who roamed the streets usually did so because they had nothing better to do. One of the most rewarding experiences for a child is to have an outlet for his creativity. If children in our community were given a variety of opportunities to be creative, we would be able to keep a large number of them off the streets and enrich their lives considerably. The boy who can successfully fulfill his creative and emotional needs has little time or reason to participate in negative behavior. Surveys by noted educators have proven that creatively fulfilled children show a marked increase in academic excellence. In an area of the city where 85 percent of students read below grade level, motivating institutions like the Boys Choir of Harlem are a matter of life and death. "What children at the Boys Choir of Harlem do is what all our children can do if we are willing to give up the time," I told another reporter.

Underlying any education on character is the issue of race. At the Boys Choir, we put principles into action. Everything that we do is a statement that we are a part of America, capable of performing Bach, Mozart, Handel, Bernstein—and performing them well. We are not racists. But we are pro-black, and everyone knows what our actions represent: "We can do this music as well as anyone. This is not somebody else's music. This is my music because I can make it my music." We do spirituals, jazz, and hip-hop. We disprove the notion that black kids are only violent and uneducated. It takes a lot of hard work, given the odds against us. People who are surprised that we know how to sing classical music have come up to me after a performance and said, "I didn't know they could sing Mozart."

Children, especially black children, must understand the realities of being black in America. They must know the history. Our children cannot simply become race-neutral. Our experiences have been different from those of white children, and in order for them to understand the present they must know their past. Race matters in 1995 just as much as it did before the Civil Rights movement. I don't want to hear that we are all the same. We are not starting from the same level. That's ridiculous. The Jews have a saying, "Never forget." We, too, must never forget our Holocaust. Far too many blacks have bought into the notion that everything is equal now and that we must go forward. There is too much history, too much baggage, and no one is color-blind.

Thirty years after the passage of the Civil Rights Act, African-Americans are for the most part still segregated and dependent upon themselves for advancement. All too often, we have not picked up the ball at a time when we need the entire village to step up and put in the time. Back when I was growing up, living in a segregated world gave blacks a sense of racial pride. Neighborhoods were filled with relatives and a mixture of professionals and blue-collar workers. Black doctors lived in one house, a black undertaker in another. The black shopkeeper lived on one side of the street, the black teacher across the way. I had role models growing up. I knew that it was all right and wonderful to be black. Children nowadays don't really have that. Most of the blacks they see in the news are committing crimes or they are on television as comedians. Don't get me wrong; America needed the federal government to ensure equal opportunity. But segregation did have a positive effect. There was a sense of community within the black neighborhoods. There was also an unshakable belief that anyone could do anything and become anybody. There was no stigma attached to being poor; poverty was not in itself a measure of potential or success.

The majority of our board members had little understanding of what is required to run an organization of both high artistic integrity and even higher social value. Their ignorance would have been almost laughable if the situation hadn't been so serious, especially considering that some of these people made decisions affecting my ability to run the organization. Several embarked on an unofficial campaign to gain control over the Boys Choir of Harlem in the late eighties that continues to this very day. They demonstrated their unfamiliarity with the choir in a number of ways. We struggled, for instance, to hire qualified part-time conductors and, once hired, keep them on staff instead of losing them to their own music careers. "Just hire another conductor," several board members said. Hiring a conductor is not like hiring an accountant. We can't simply go to a business school and select from a pool of generally qualified and eager people. Our requirements are much different and less quantifiable. There are certain skills that are obviously needed, but there are intangibles that are equally important, such as the ability to fit in. We have a family in which the students and staff are devoted to each other. Everyone is like kinfolks. The energy level is high, the commitment total.

After our run on Broadway, where we had performed night after night, matinee after matinee, for two straight weeks, I told a board member during a meeting that the show was tiring and the boys were exhausted. "But they're having fun," the board member said. "It's just fun stuff." It wasn't so much the comment but the baggage that came along with the comment: the total lack of understanding of the work involved to prepare for performances. The board's ignorance put an incredible burden on our ability to produce artistically. Very few of the members understood the work involved to take a show on the road. The pressure caused divisions among the staff, with some choosing to take sides with the board. The split created an unpleasant work atmosphere, which over time, also took its toll. A lot of our hardest workers became burned out.

The clash with the board was inevitable. Most members have no background in the arts or in running social programs. They have raised paltry amounts of money, despite our international stature. The kids are doing their jobs. They raise about a third of our $3 million budget. Instead of fund-raising, the board has involved itself, in many instances, with the day-to-day operations of the choir and tried to mold the choir based upon their limited understanding of what it needs to perform on a world-class level. The choir is not like a business that sells nuts and bolts. We are dealing with children as students and performers; both endeavors are strongly linked to one another. The board doesn't quite understand the relationship and is more concerned with money, or in our case, the lack of money.

Before the friction with the board began four years ago, most of the staff was committed, giving 110 percent to a job they loved. The pressures were there only because of the type of work we were involved in. There was pressure to take the children on tour; it was extremely difficult dealing with challenging children, their lives further complicated by serious family and emotional problems. The board appeared annoyed at our problems. Instead of recognizing that all nonprofits had deficits during the late eighties and early nineties—many of them had even gone bankrupt and out of business—the board simply blamed a lack of management structure.

The battles with the board were costly. Steve Pane resigned. He told me that he was just too burned out. For the first time, he hated his job. Usually he felt that he was too busy or that he was under too much pressure. But the board had caused him to actually hate something that I knew he loved. He had wanted to run his own choir and eventually found a choir director's job at a small college in Maine. His departure meant a double loss—his wife also worked at the Boys Choir of Harlem. She had chaired our piano department and was fluent in Japanese. When we went to Japan for the second time back in 1989, she taught the boys about Japanese culture and language. They got the biggest kick out of that and were able to greet some of their fans in their native language.

Fortunately, we were able to hire an alumnus to step in for Pane—Roger Holland. We had come full circle, and seeing Roger accept a leadership role made me think less of the troubles with the board and more of the future of the choir. He began by teaching music theory and worked his way up to become the director of artistic education. He saw the choir from a new angle. He was now teaching some of his former colleagues and gained a deeper understanding of our mission. He realized how blessed he was to have parents that took the time to discipline him and make sure that he had home training. He saw that a lot of the kids didn't have that kind of parents.

"You have to impart a lot of social values to these kids, helping them to garner what's important and helping them to learn how to prioritize," he told me. "You have to affect their world view and how they see things. You have to help them shape their thought process. Traveling with the choir helps them. Their view becomes more worldly, not so localized and one-sided. They learn that things don't necessarily have to be one way and that their way is not the only way. Things can be done differently, for different reasons."

Teachers never know which of their students will turn out to be the one child who sat in class and absorbed everything that was offered. One such student was Leon Williams. After he left the boys choir in 1983, he graduated from Westminster Choir College and would receive a master's degree from the Juilliard in 1991. He is presently on tour as a baritone, giving recitals in New York and in Japan. He has also won prestigious music awards, including the Lola Wilson Hayes Vocal Award. To makes ends meet, he works at the Grand Tier Restaurant at the Metropolitan Opera House. He is twenty-nine years old now. He is not able to make a full-time living yet from his singing, but he is progressing. On occasion, he receives a nice-size fee for a performance. His patience is his strength; he refuses to spend a lot of time pondering the frustrations inherent in the music business. He simply puts his head down and tries to plow through. We have stayed in touch over the years, and I am particularly proud of him.

I remember watching his debut recital at Merkin Concert Hall near Lincoln Center. His artistry was excellent, and my chest almost exploded with pride.

He always tried to do his best, not willing to accept second-best. Williams sang with his church choir in Brooklyn during his freshman year in high school. Donna Brown, the organist who would later bring Roger Holland to the choir, invited Williams to an audition. He had a lovely voice and started attending rehearsals. His family was very supportive. His father worked as a welder; his mother was an elementary school teacher and music director at a church. He had three older brothers.

"When I first walked in I wasn't at a very high level of musicianship at all," he told me. "I sang and performed by rote in church choirs, and here it was just a totally different atmosphere. It was completely professional, first-rate, world-class music-making from the beginning of the approach all the way to the performance and the applause. I mean, you got to really experience firsthand the way professional musicians prepare a score. At first it was a little

. . . I wouldn't say intimidating . . . but it was just very enlightening to see how that process worked when you were handed a score that was more than two pages long—a complete oratorio, for instance—and you realized that by the end of this projected period, you would have mastered that piece of music. I have to admit that before that a song to me was words on a piece of paper, and occasionally a hymn book. But coming here was really my first encounter with major classical scores and dissecting them, then making an interpretive presentation."

Williams said that it wasn't one thing in particular about the boys choir that stuck with him over the years. "It was the entire process," he told me. "Living a life and studying music on such a high level was part of it. We were not made to feel less-than just because we didn't have certain tools. We knew we were getting those tools and were getting that experience. World-class singers would come and work with us, conductors would come, and you knew that this was real; it's not something where you were being disillusioned into thinking you were a great musician. You knew that you were a student and not as advanced. But you also knew there was some common ground with the professional musicians, that you were on a level that was high enough to be associated with these artists.

"I just saw things very romantically and spiritually, and I always just felt a connection," Williams went on. "It didn't matter what Turnbull said. There was just a certain passion that you got when you were there, and the energy was such that he was able to conduct before he even lifted a baton. I was a very strong-headed youngster, too, and I wouldn't go to things and stick around if I didn't feel like it was something worthwhile. I knew from the first day that I was at BCH that this would be something to commit myself to."

The challenge kept Williams energized. "It's so easy, especially when you're living in the city and going to public schools, to take a rest, to go home, watch television, and not participate in any extracurriculars. But this was something that was challenging not only on an academic level but on a personal level. I had to ask myself: do I want to make the commitment, do I want to be ten times as exhausted as I normally would be when I'm done with a day at school, do I want to take myself as far as I can possibly go? There was a lot of decision-making that had to take place at a very early age. It forced you to do that because there was never any arm twisting. I can remember Turnbull saying, 'You can have the world if you work for it.' I viewed it very spiritually. That's why I was always able to absorb and take in everything that he gave. I can't give you one thing that he said that sparked me to go on. It was just when you walked in you knew that his energy was there, and you wanted to emulate that in your own commitment and in your own involvement." Williams wasn't a great student; he maintained a B average. He was a self-described "music monster," spending most of his time reading biographies of great singers and attending concerts and performances.

"The attention that Turnbull gave to us individually was so selfless," he said. "Everyone always criticized him for not having a life, but it was just something that had to have been rewarding for him because people were growing and people were changing for the better. The only word I can use is passion, because it was always there. Never did I see him losing faith or losing hope; he was always just breathing an energy that meant you had to get off your ass and work.

"There were some things that made it easy and some

that made it more challenging," he explained. "The things that made it very easy was that with gospel music it was ninety-nine percent interpretive and expressive and communicative. You were basically relaying Scriptures or relaying a pious idea about Jesus or God or struggle or pain or glory. Gospel was easy after you struggled with the confined aspect of the classical literature or the restrictive aspect, rather, where you couldn't really take off and make up your own notes. That's what was most difficult at the beginning. You could go into a performance singing gospel or even pop and just say, 'Oh you know, when I feel it I'll just let it out.' But the demands were so much greater in classical to perform exactly what was on the page, plus interpret within those guidelines, to make something human within the guidelines of the black-and-white notes on the page.

"My education here was almost backwards in a way," he said. "Turnbull put the cart before the horse. He took on young, untrained students, untrained children, and put them on a world-class concert stage. Even though we had classes on sight-reading and piano and language, the focus was always the concert. In a different setting where you were training children, you might not always focus on the concert because you knew that you had to get a foundation going that would eventually equip that student with what he needed for a concert career. But here, it was always a major focus on that performance and being good enough for the performance choir. The concerts made it real. It made the rehearsals worthwhile. I can't imagine any one boy, whether he was interested in being a musician or not, standing up there on a huge platform in the middle of a festival in Germany with thousands of people screaming and yelling and clapping, and not getting a sense of satisfaction that was beyond compare.

"That's the feeling that you get, because it's not rare for youngsters to be well trained and to be world traveled, and to be well educated," he said. "The rare thing is for youngsters who are typically and unfortunately stereotypically impoverished, low-income, not motivated, not inspired, from broken homes, and definitely not from families of great classical music culture to be able to perform so beautifully and so exceptionally. You just knew that something like this was not supposed to be taking place in the middle of the city, where there were budget cuts and schools that were falling apart. It wasn't just the superficial life of being on the stage. It was the fact that we had come to a point where we knew we had something worthwhile to offer. It was like something you had to show off because you were doubtful at first, you gave it a shot, you worked hard, it manifested itself into something great, and with that achievement came the desire to want to show it off."

In order to keep our standards at this level, we had to figure out ways to bring in more revenue. Two years ago, we developed a specific strategy to make the Boys Choir of Harlem a commercial success on a limited basis. Because we had such a very fine artistic entity that received major fees all over the world, we decided upon three goals: a Broadway show, an album, and a movie. If successful, we thought, the Boys Choir of Harlem could continue to provide services that are mostly paid for by the work of the children. To a large degree, our strategy was the brainchild of one man—Barry Rosenthal.

Rosenthal, a Boston entertainment attorney, helped develop the pop group New Kids on the Block into a major sensation during the late eighties. Without a doubt, he was one of those people who had a great deal of love for choir and respect for me. He pulled together a group of people in the entertainment industry and set up a marketing committee. He started making things happen. The first was Broadway. In 1994, we had a two-week run at the Richard Rodgers Theatre. The show was called *The Boys Choir of Harlem and Friends, Live on Broadway*, and, indeed, we had the help of a lot of our friends to pull it off. Geoffrey Holder choreographed the show, and countless musicians and singers performed with us, including Michael Bolton, Juanita Fleming, Carmen Dellavalade, and Ronald Richardson, to name a few. The shows were hot, and to my knowledge, no other boys choir in the world has ever had their own run on Broadway. Even though we didn't make as much money as we had anticipated, the engagement was a major success in that it gave the choir unprecedented exposure and commercial viability.

We started planning for the development of an album shortly after our run on Broadway. The choir was not unfamiliar with working in a studio. We had already appeared on the soundtracks for the hit movies *Glory* in 1989, *Jungle Fever*, in 1991, and *Malcolm X* in 1992. We also appeared on several well-known artists' albums: as background vocalists on Mandy Patinkin's *Dress Casual*; as solo artists with Dianne Reeves, James Williams, Tony Reedus, and Peter Washington on Blue Note's *Christmas Carols and Sacred Songs*; and as featured artists on *Michael Crawford Performs Andrew Lloyd Webber*; Florence Quivar's *Ride On, King Jesus*; Quincy Jones's *Handel's Messiah: A Soulful Celebration*; Glen Campbell's *Wings of Victory*; Kathleen Battle's *A Christmas Celebration*; James Ingram's *Always You*; and Alvin and the Chipmunks' *A Very Merry Chipmunk*.

Having our own album, however, was a first. We spent several months in the studio to produce *A Song of Hope* for Atlantic East/West records.

So many great opportunities have presented themselves over the years. Take the movie *Glory*. It started out as simply one in a series of things that people call and ask us to do. We spent four days on the Lorimar soundstage in Hollywood. It was great, and as I recall, Sylvester Stallone signed autographs for the boys. Another call came for us to open for Luciano Pavarotti during his special in 1994. Millions of people saw the special on television, broadcast live nationwide on the Public Broadcasting Service, and an estimated 500,000 fans crowded Central Park to watch and listen to the tenor. Pavarotti sang for about an hour. We performed several spirituals and jazz tunes during one of his breaks. Another telephone call came from Eddie Murphy. He asked us to be on his record *What's Up with You?* We were in Hollywood again, this time on the Paramount soundstage. It wasn't that much work, but the exposure was great. While there, we also performed in a video with Michael Jackson, who was also on Murphy's record. And yet another call came from Kurt Masur, conductor of the New York Philharmonic Orchestra. He has scheduled performances for the choir in 1996 with the orchestra. He also wants to take us to Europe.

All of our appearances are important in putting the Boys Choir of Harlem on another level. The media coverage, especially stories on television, helped solidify in the public's mind that the choir was special. *60 Minutes* was one of the highlights of our entire career because it captivated a whole group of people that we would have never been able to reach. CBS played the segment three years straight. I still have people now who tell me that they come to concerts because they saw the *60 Minutes* piece.

The choir has been an inspiration, and as such, Barry Rosenthal thought it would make a powerful subject for a big-screen movie. He had the ear of Hollywood. He had represented Errol Morris, director of *The Thin Blue Line*, and Pat Conroy, author of *Prince of Tides*. Unfortunately, Rosenthal had a heart attack and died during the middle of negotiations with the Walt Disney Company in September 1994. His loss was devastating. He was totally committed to the choir and very much concerned about me. In fact, he took it upon himself to see that I could receive a raise, something that the board had not talked about in ten years. He told me constantly how upset he was about the board's inability to see the amount of work that the choir required of me. Just managing the one hundred or so performances a year is a full-time job. Rosenthal was a true friend. We eventually landed a movie deal with Disney, my brother Horace and Rosenthal's partner completing the negotiations. Our relationship with Walt Disney does not stop with the movie. Last June, we appeared at the grand opening of their movie *Pocahontas*. We were introduced as the "pride of New York."

Our journey continues to be a bumpy ride, lurching from tragedy to triumph, the problems never ending, the solutions slow in coming. Performing onstage is almost a relief; getting there is often filled with unpredictable problems. Nevertheless, the road trips are where everything comes together: all the rehearsals, all the discipline, all the counseling and school work. Once we are onstage, everything is fine. It's getting there that presents untold problems.

One recent sixteen-day tour through the Midwest began in Nashville and ended in Minnesota, with thirteen concerts in between. The trip began at La Guardia Airport. Forty-six boys, all members of the performing choir, stood near the gate in rows of two. I handed them their tickets as they walked down the gangway, and collected them when they found their seats. One eight-year-old had forgotten his backpack. Frank helped him find it and talked with him, gently, about responsibility and how he had to keep up with his things. The boy shook his head and found his seat, relieved that he had not lost a possession before leaving New York. Of course, when we arrived in Nashville, another child would forget to pick up one of his bags from the baggage area. And Frank gave him, too, a lecture on responsibility.

As with every tour, we like to make a few announcements once we arrive in the city and are in a relatively quiet place. On this particular tour, the first announcements were made on the the bus we hired.

"Welcome, everyone, to the spring tour," Frank began. One person clapped. "I'm glad to know that we have at least one happy camper on hand." One by one, each of the boys began clapping, until the sound was thunderous. "That's better," Frank said.

He introduced the new tutors: one for grades five through seven, and another for grades nine through eleven. Frank next introduced the driver of the bus and christened him the new "director of transportation."

It's time to get down to business, Frank said. "We are going to have school every day. It is important to know what is going on at all times. You have an itinerary where we break down the schedule, city by city. Everyone should know how long the bus ride is from one city to another in order to regulate energy.

"Also, we have changed the seating arrangements,"

Frank went on. "The trebles usually sit in the back, but because they are so talkative, we have decided to move them up next to Dr. Turnbull. We have also changed some of the room assignments. Each room will have three people and a team captain. The team captain is responsible for making sure their roommates are where they are supposed to be when they are supposed to be there."

As Frank read the room assignments, some of the boys began yelling "yes" upon hearing to whom they were assigned. The noise became troublesome. On one level it was becoming increasingly loud. On another, it was making some children feel unwanted. I rose from my seat in the front of the bus very slowly, my face stern, my lips tight. The kids immediately quieted. I sat back down without saying a word. It's about setting ground rules. If we let kids do anything that they want, then they will do anything within their personalities. We have to set the ground rules, the parameters, to let them work within that framework. Generally, they will stay within the limits. Some of our critics will say that we give our children too much freedom. But even freedom has rules. Yes, we are free. But we don't go around and spit in people's faces. There are certain responsibilities associated with freedom. We are gracious. We say "hello," "good morning," "thank you" and "please."

We arrived at the hotel around 9:30 P.M. Of course, the boys were hungry again. The hotel's restaurant had closed. The only food left was junk from the vending machines and hot chocolate, tea, and coffee at the hotel's snack bar. Most of the boys like to laugh at the band's guitarist, Ayodele. But at times like these, he has the last laugh. He carries a large black leather backpack. But instead of clothes, he carries several large plastic Ziploc plastic bags containing all sorts of health food—oats, raisins, coconuts, molasses.

He went to the snack bar, and instead of drinking a cup of hot chocolate, he pulled out a bowl, poured in some oats, raisins, and hot water, and had a bowl of oatmeal. "Nashville has a good vibe," he said. "It's a very musical place."

The peace became unglued during our town meeting. After the boys put their belongings in their rooms, I asked them to come downstairs to the hotel lobby in order to go over a few more details about the tour. In the past, we told the boys their travel schedules on a day-by-day basis. On this trip, we tried something new. We gave them the schedule for the entire sixteen-day trip. "We want to pass out a few announcements that are designed to keep you informed as to when we will have school and when you will have particular classes. We'll have study periods that are forty-five minutes in length; we will have a change of periods, the same as we do in our regular school. There will be a system for announcing when one period ends and another period begins. The key thing about each of these sessions is that every minute has to be used productively. We really do not have time for joking, for the divergent activities when someone decides they want to be humorous or whatever. In other words, this is not the time to hone or sharpen any of your comedic skills; it's so that you can go back to school feeling confident, feeling secure that you'll have something of quality to present to your teachers. Everyone has to be his own decision-maker. I want you to study the itinerary. None of you can afford television. It's a waste of energy. When you start performing you will run out of gas because you didn't get proper rest. We have an intense travel schedule. I don't want anyone, especially our little candles, burning out too soon. I don't want to hear people complaining about being tired or sick. You must use your time and energy wisely."

Frank asked how many of the boys brought their books with them. Everyone nodded their heads as if they had. Frank proceeded by talking about the study hall schedules. He then asked one boy if he had his books and if he could see them. The boy didn't have any of his books. Frank, still understanding and patient, let the boys know that he was extremely disappointed. "You don't have your books," he told the boy. "I was saying to myself when I saw that raggedy book bag of yours looking like it had come from a starving nation, 'There can't be any books in that bag. It's so empty looking. He must have gotten robbed on the plane. The book bag looked so empty. It couldn't possibly be a book bag of a student.'"

The boy was asked to sit down at his table in the back of the lobby. "This just doesn't cut it," Frank said. "I want each of you to level with me. How did you think you were going to do the work?" I heard Frank's voice from the other side of the lobby and came over to discover what was happening. Several of the boys had left their books at home. They struck deals with one another to share each other's books in order to avoid carrying a heavy load with them.

"Are you kidding?" I asked the boys. "This is not acceptable. It's not even discussable. It's so irresponsible. This trip has started on the wrong foot. I see now that you will not be responsible. You must treat your schoolwork like your music. Not bringing your books is like thinking that somebody next to you would know the words to the song. But that's not good enough. The choir sounds half good. Some of you think that when we go on the road, that this will be Club Med or something. Some of your teachers may be accepting of these lame excuses. But not me. That doesn't cut it with me. Oh to be slick: and many of you thought that we wouldn't check. That is exactly why we hold these town meetings. Here we are sitting in the middle of nowhere and these kids don't have the basic tools. We might as well be on the moon."

One boy said his friend told him that he would bring his Spanish book. "Well, is he going to sing your part for you during the performance?" I snapped. "It's no wonder that when you get back, you are accustomed to doing shoddy work. And when you don't know what you are learning, you find yourself talking and being disruptive."

Frank came up with a great question. "How many of you brought Walkmen and didn't bring their books?" Frank asked. About a dozen boys raised their hands. "Well, I want each of you to go to your rooms and bring those Walkmen down here. You will get them back when we get back to New York." I also added a new requirement. "Once we figure out which books we have, those who do not have their books for a particular class will have to pay to make copies of those pages. If you run out of spending money, then too bad."

We performed at the Ryman Auditorium the next night. The building was the original home of the Grand Ole Opry, before it moved to Opryland. Ryman had been recently restored by the city of Nashville after it had been shut down for twenty years. The Boys Choir of Harlem were the first African-Americans to appear there since Marian Anderson on January 20, 1943. The twenty-one-hundred-seat hall was nearly full, and for many blacks in the audience, it was the first time they had ever been inside this place where country music had taken flight; where Patsy Cline belted her longings, Roy Acuff unleashed his "Wabash Cannonball," and Uncle Dave Macon played his banjo like a "monkey handles a peanut," as the saying went. Hank Williams played there and Booker T. Washington once gave a speech in the hall. The interior had been restored to its original condition. The handcrafted oak pews harkened back to the days when the Ryman was a tabernacle. Gothic columns supported the balcony. Stained-glass windows created a kaleidoscope of light. We opened with Haydn's *Te Deum*, followed by Brahms's *Zigeunerlieder.* The crowd was appreciative; their applause wonderful. Before the next musical selection, I talked with the audience for a minute.

"Good evening," I said.

The audience gave a limp response.

"C'mon folks, it ain't that stuffy," I told them. "These boys may look like they are angels, but I can assure you, they are not. If you could ride the bus with them, or be in the same hotel with them, you'd know what I mean. Now, good evening."

"*Good evening,*" the audience responded.

"That's better," I said, laughing.

Not all of the children who have come to the Boys Choir of Harlem are angels. In fact we have had more than our share of knuckleheads. But their hard work has touched millions of people across the world. It's the soul of these young men connecting with the music, their voices transcending all races and cultures. We expect the most from our kids, and in return, we get their best. It's easy to write off these children, as so many do. Our building is located on 128th Street and Madison Avenue, and near the back of our school lie the commuter rail lines. I often watch those trains go by, carrying passengers back and forth from the suburbs to the city, seemingly oblivious of the lives underneath the rusty trestles. Ironically, one of the trains is called the North Star. If its passengers only knew the joy of Harlem. We are a song of hope. We have an unwavering faith that we shall triumph over any adversity. We know that these children, who walk past drug dealers, murderers, and prostitutes everyday, can be anything they choose. The applause and ovations after performances provide the confirmation; letters from the boys are the ultimate testament to our work:

JIMMIE K. KIMBROUGH

Being a member of the choir is something I carry with honor. You're like an ambassador of Harlem and the positive things that Harlem has to offer. That's a lot for a teenager, but we are capable of upholding our position. The choir has taught me that tomorrow is not promised, so use your time wisely. One of the biggest things the choir has taught me is how to adapt to different situations. This can be applied on the stage and in everyday living. Respecting different cultures and people who may not do things that I do is stressed in the choir a lot. The choir has prepared me for the real world and I know how competitive it is, but being a member of the choir, you have to compete for a spot in the touring choir every day. Three hundred boys fighting for thirty-five spots to sing is competitive, so the real world is being drilled in us every day at the choir so when the time comes when I'm on my own, I'll be prepared.

In my eight years at the choir, Turnbull has been my mentor, a father and someone that you can talk to about anything. Like myself, a lot of members have single parents and Dr. Turnbull fills that gap. He's on you twenty-four seven and always brings the best out of someone. Turnbull is always talking about reaching the next level, even when you feel like you can't get any better.

TYREE MARCUS

What it means to be a member of the Boys Choir of Harlem to me is being a well-rounded person, meaning you have to be honest, trustworthy, responsible, and a leader. Growing up in the choir I've learned such values like discipline, meaning being able to carry yourself in a proper and cordial manner. The choir has also taught me about honesty and courage, meaning that you stand up for doing the right things instead of the wrong ones. The choir has done that by always being involved in my life. What the choir has taught me about life is that when you grow up things are going to be hard, so we have to start young and get an education so that when we get older things will be easier. Dr. Turnbull has been helpful in my life by being a father figure, a role model, and someone to look up to. If it wasn't for him and some of the other teachers, I don't know what I'd be doing.

GREGORY ROUNTREE

The choir has taught me a lot since I've been here. But it has truly shown me about the real world. Trying to give me the skills that I need to make the grade in the world. I've been taught by the choir how to express myself onstage and offstage. I've always been afraid to talk and to express myself to people, females especially. But with the choir I have gotten over that fear of talking to people. And that just makes me more of the young man that I am today. For values, like discipline, honesty and courage. I've already been taught them by my mother and father. But the choir has just reinforced these values even more. And it's only been able to do that through Dr. Turnbull. For without all of his strict actions, many of our values would not be straight. And maybe some of us wouldn't have any. Since I've been in the choir, Dr. Turnbull has been a teacher in my life. Teaching me music and about life. He has helped me to develop knowledge of different people and different cultures. Next to my father, he is a great man in my book. Even though both of them sometimes get on my nerves. But I still love and respect them both for the big impact they have made on my life.

TRAVEL PRICE

Dr. Turnbull likes a lot of discipline. That's one of the things he has taught me. I can stand still for an hour straight without moving. He also taught me courage and to respect other people. I can talk to people and ask them questions without being afraid to talk to people I don't even know. I used to be a baby and cry every time I got in trouble, but when I get in trouble now I just have to do what he says. He also taught me to sing different varieties of songs like classical, spiritual, pop, rap, gospel.

ALEX ORTIZ

When I walk down the street and friends ask me what school I go to, I'm proud to say Boys Choir of Harlem Academy. Boys Choir of Harlem is world renowned, therefore it cannot be judged against a lot of other schools. The choir does not only teach music and education but it prepares you for life. As we travel to many places in the world, we learn about people and lifestyles. We learn how to adapt to many places. I've learned that the world is not easy on black and Latino youth. The choir has taught me life is what you make of it. Through music the choir has taught me about values such as honesty and self-discipline.

Honesty is not only needed in music but in your life. You must be honest with yourself. You must also have discipline. If you can't act right, who's going to want to work with you? No one likes uncontrollable people. Respect is another value which the choir has taught me. When I was younger I did not respect myself. I now not only respect myself but I respect others around me. I owe a lot to the people in the choir.

Even though they could be doing something else, they are here donating their time to be with us. You might say, giving back to the community. Mr. Jones, our guidance counselor, has been helpful in my life. He's there for us. He's like the guardian angel. I've had many hard times in the choir even when I had to fight some people. If I can't calm myself down I'll talk to Mr. Jones and he'll give me advice. Dr. Turnbull has also been very helpful to me. Sometimes he could be very hard on me, but he wouldn't be hard on me if he didn't care. Dr. Turnbull usually is very blunt and to the point. That is just one quality that I admire. If he doesn't like it, he'll say "I hate it" and he won't stop until he gets it right. He's sort of a perfectionist. I also admire him for succeeding in life when the odds were against him. Even though his life was hard, he made it to college and made something out of himself. For that, I give him a lot of respect and admiration.

KERON GRAHAM

Being a part of the choir is an honor. The choir has teachers that care about your life so much. The teachers work at the choir because they like their jobs or the kids. People don't laugh at other people when a person says something or sings something wrong. The Boys Choir of Harlem teaches me a lot about life, like when you do something wrong and somebody asks you did you do it, tell them the truth; don't let someone tell you what to do all the time; you have to think for yourself sometimes. The choir taught me discipline by when they go to places and when they say go somewhere you have to go. When you have to control yourself and stop moving that is discipline. The choir has been able to do that by having talks, too, and on the road they take time out to have talks about being disciplined, honest, and being a good adult. Dr. Turnbull has been helpful in my life by teaching me how to be a great young man, when to have fun and when to control myself when it is time to do work. Dr. Turnbull has made a change in my life.

KERON NIXON

It really means a lot because if it wasn't for the choir I just might be some little hardheaded kid running the streets. The choir has taught me that in order to be a real man in the future you have to have discipline, manners, etc. Yes I do think that the choir has taught me about the values of life that await me. I think that the choir was able to do that because they are strong, caring people that are willing to improve the lives of people. First of all, Dr. Turnbull is one of those caring people, but he's greater than all of them because he is like the hardest worker of them all and I give my respects.

ALLEN PINKNEY

This new routine with all the discipline was really a change for me. Before coming to the choir I wasn't used to being still and concentrating for a long time. Also I got the freedom to ride the bus from the Bronx all by myself. My father, who is a fire prevention systems inspector, and my mother, who is a homemaker, were really glad that I was getting some discipline and learning to calm down. I made it through all of the hard work and I thought it was over but it had just begun. As I became a performing choir member, I began to see what the choir was really about. I saw how the staff tried to help us in all aspects of our lives to better ourselves. I never really understood why Dr. Turnbull would scream and yell at us. At times I thought he hated us, but as time went on and I began to realize my situation as a black boy growing into a man in America, I began to see he cared, because if he didn't care he wouldn't stay on us. I have had many different experiences with the choir, but the most important and lasting ones were my opportunities to travel and experience other cultures and learn to respect other ways of life. Through my travels I realized as a poor boy from the Bronx that there is life outside of the Bronx. There are better lives and some are worse. These experiences helped me to realize that the world doesn't revolve around me and the Bronx. One of the major things the choir has taught me is discipline that hopefully will stick with me for life. That is one way the music has transcended into every aspect of my life. I'm able to travel all over the world and still get good grades in school because of prayer and discipline. Through discipline the choir and the staff have conveyed to me that as a black man in America, excellence is the only way to be successful in spite of racism. Excellence, excellence is what the choir means to me.

Bibliography

A brief note on research: There is a wealth of material published on the state of Mississippi, the Civil Rights movement, Harlem and education in general, and the teaching of values in particular. The following books were incredibly useful in filling the blanks in my own recollections of growing up during such a tumultuous time and providing insight into teaching young men and women how to think and do the right thing.

Aptheker, Herbert. *A Documentary History of the Negro People in the United States.* Vol. 6, *From the Korean War to the Emergence of Martin Luther King, Jr.* New York: Carol Publishing Group, 1993.

Branch, Taylor. *Parting the Waters: America in the King Years 1954–63.* New York: Simon & Schuster, 1988.

Campbell, Clarice T., and Oscar Allan Rogers, Jr. *Mississippi: The View from Tougaloo.* Jackson, Miss.: University Press of Mississippi, 1979.

Grant, Gerald. *The World We Created at Hamilton High.* Cambridge, Mass.: Harvard University Press, 1988.

Grant, Joanne. *Black Protest: History, Documents and Analyses, 1619 to the Present.* New York: Ballantine, 1968.

Greenberg, Jack. *Crusaders in the Courts.* New York: HarperCollins, 1994.

Lemann, Nicholas. *The Promised Land: The Great Migration and How It Changed America.* New York: Alfred A. Knopf, 1991.

Keating, Bern. *History of Washington County.* Greenville, Miss.: Greenville Junior Auxiliary, 1976.

Moody, Anne. *Coming of Age in Mississippi.* New York: Dell, 1968.

Nossiter, Adam. *Of Long Memory: Mississippi and the Murder of Medgar Evers.* Reading, Mass.: Addison-Wesley, 1994.

Powledge, Fred. *Free at Last? The Civil Rights Movement and the People Who Made It.* Boston: Little, Brown, 1991.

Sansing, David G., and Carroll Waller. *A History of the Mississippi Governor's Mansion.* Jackson, Miss.: University Press of Mississippi, 1977.

Sizer, Theodore R. *Horace's Compromise: The Dilemma of the American High School.* Boston: Houghton Mifflin, 1984.

Taulbert, Clifford L. *When We Were Colored.* Tulsa, Okla.: Council Oak Books, 1989.

Thomas, Emory M. *The Confederate Nation, 1861–1865.* New York: Harper and Row, 1979.

Wagner, Tony. *How Schools Change: Lessons from Three Communities.* Boston: Beacon Press, 1994.

Wilkins, Roy, with Tom Mathews. *Standing Fast: The Autobiography of Roy Wilkins.* New York: Da Capa Press, 1982.

Keys to success at the Boys Choir of Harlem:

We have found that our success has been largely the result of establishing basic codes of conduct and enforcing those standards with diligence and rigor. We do not overlook what may appear obvious. These simple goals lead to strong moral foundations. Their beauty lies in their simplicity. The difficult part is finding educators and parents who are willing to provide the level of commitment, dedication, and energy to keep the children on the right track.

1. *K*eep an open mind to constructive criticism. Even the best constantly seek ways to improve and are not completely satisfied with praise only.

2. *K*now your surroundings and act accordingly. We want our children to behave with class and dignity everywhere they go. We also want them to understand the differences in having class at the White House and having class at a neighborhood playground. Rude and discourteous behavior, however, is not acceptable anywhere.

3. *T*rust your own judgments, make your own decisions. Following the crowd is often the easy way out; leaders listen to their own hearts and minds.

4. *B*e honest with others and, more important, yourself.

5. *S*et goals and complete them. The combination of talent,

discipline, and hard work is unbeatable. No one gets something for nothing.

6. Be prepared for the unexpected. Life is filled with surprises and disappointments; the ability to adapt and bounce back are vital for long-range success.

7. Be a team player. The part is never greater than the whole, and a selfish attitude gets in the way of progress.

8. Develop and appreciate high standards. The goal is excellence—there is no substitute.